Getting the Buggers to Add Up

Second Edition

Related titles:

100 Ideas for Teaching Mathematics – Mike Ollerton
Inclusive Mathematics 11–18 – Mike Ollerton and Anne Watson
Teaching Number Sense – Julia Anghileri
Teaching Maths using ICT 2nd Edition – Adrian Oldknow and
   Ron Taylor
Learning Mathematics 3rd Edition – Anthony Orton
Teaching and Learning Algebra – Doug French
Teaching and Learning Geometry – Doug French

Getting the Buggers to Add Up

Second Edition

MIKE OLLERTON

continuum

Continuum International Publishing Group
The Tower Building 80 Maiden Lane
11 York Road Suite 704
London SE1 7NX New York
  NY 10038

www.continuumbooks.com

British Library Cataloguing-in-Publication Data
A catalogue record for this book is available from the British Library.

ISBN: 0–8264–8914–1 (paperback)

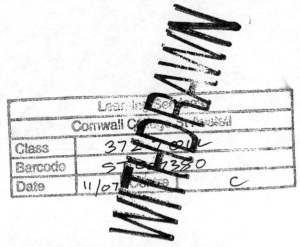

Typeset by BookEns Ltd, Royston, Herts.
Printed and bound in Great Britain by
Antony Rowe Ltd, Chippenham, Wiltshire

Daily miracles

To achieve daily miracles, teachers build up marvellous inter-personal communication skills. We build sound relationships and construct classroom environments where mutual respect exists. We devise whole ranges of strategies and ways of responding to the plethora of situations we face day by day in schools. Interactions are unpredictable. Something happens and action has to be taken. There is no recipe or guidebook to tell us how to make on-the-spot decisions, to explain what to say, how to say it or how to act. There is no substitute for experience. However, experience alone is not a sufficient condition to guarantee development of expertise. It is through a teacher's ability to reflect upon, make sense of and rationalize experience that we develop our inner strength and make sense of the enormous complexity of being a teacher. Through experience we learn how to take the heat out of situations, when to step in and when to stand aside. We learn to be strategic, when to notice explicitly what is going on and when to ignore certain other events in classrooms. It is not mere luck, therefore, that the vast majority of classrooms are safe, supportive and respectful places where effective and affective learning occurs, based upon positive relationships and interesting ideas.

Education is constantly under the spotlight of the media and is used (and abused) by politicians as a vehicle for pursuing the vote-catching agenda. We deal not only with all kinds of events and situations concerning students, but also with colleagues, parents, inspectors and the uninvited wasp that flies in. Certain events, and our responses to them, may be predictable, but many are not and we often have to think fast and respond speedily. There's a lovely line from the film *Butch Cassidy and the Sundance Kid*. Sundance is being tested on his ability to hit a target, but initially 'fails' this test because the prescribed conditions means he has to stand still. Moments later and as a consequence of being able to 'move', he successfully performs the task, glibly suggesting 'I'm better when I move'. My point is that much of what we do as teachers is on the move and of the moment and this requires us to develop skills based upon intuition and

2

Contents

v

Acknowledgements

My thanks go to Alexandra Webster for suggesting I could write this book and to Christina Parkinson (also at Continuum) for her invaluable editorial comments and for providing me with necessary reality checks. My thanks also go to Catherine Sykes (Deputy Headteacher, Gawthorpe High School, Burnley) and Sue Pope (Senior Lecturer, St Martin's College, Lancaster). Both Catherine and Sue, in different ways, helped me tighten up my writing, pointed out my split infinitives, made my writing more mathematically accurate ... and sorted out my spelling!

decision-making. There are important parallels here with assessment, and about the kinds of conditions that enable students to show the best they can do – conditions which are not necessarily sitting still doing a test.

The effectiveness of decisions we make will largely be determined by the type of atmosphere we seek to create in our classrooms, and by what we learn from our experiences. My experience tells me that seeking to grab students' attention, to gain interest and to act upon natural inquisitiveness by offering problems and puzzles are key aspects of constructing a positive classroom atmosphere. Recognizing the crucial impact that the atmosphere in a classroom has upon the quality of learning cannot be understated, and this is an issue permeating the whole of this book. However, before leaving this issue of classroom atmosphere. I offer the following thought about listing the key elements which frame or describe one's classroom atmosphere; being explicit about what forms the atmosphere can be an incredibly valuable exercise. Recognizing the importance of trust; of students taking responsibility; of teacher honesty; of one's idiosyncrasies, such as being slightly crazy (speaking personally); of the value of display work; and the way visitors are greeted are examples of the kind of elements I believe are integral to classroom atmosphere. The importance of creating classrooms based upon challenge and interest cannot be understated. If the opinions of the group of Learning Support Assistants with whom I had the great pleasure of working are anything to go by, then providing students with interesting ideas to work with has a crucial impact upon behaviour ... *everything is connected*. The quote from Sotto at the beginning of this chapter is important in terms of recognizing that what happens in classrooms is strongly determined by a plethora of interconnected conditions and circumstances.

This book is therefore about teaching mathematics based upon the central theme that *everything is connected*. To this end I offer a spider diagram listing a range of issues that impact upon teaching and learning. The empty box at the bottom is to signify incompleteness, and readers might like to think about how they would fill it in.

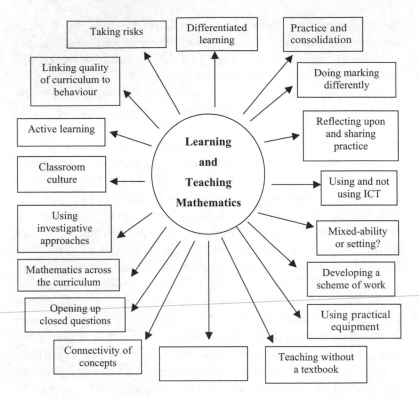

This diagram is not intended to be a comprehensive list, but it is a start. All the issues displayed are developed in this book; some appear several times in different contexts, some have specific sections or chapters attributed to them.

Structure of the book

This book is written in four main sections. Section One, together with this Introduction, explores the nature of mathematics and why anyone should wish to learn it. Section Two is about contexts and ideas for classrooms – the strategies and resources a teacher might use to support students' engagement with mathematics. Section Three considers some of the wider issues that impact upon teachers and teaching mathematics. In Section

Four I fly a few kites, and invite readers to consider the possibility and desirability of doing some things differently.

Throughout the book, ideas are offered for possible use in mathematics classrooms. I am acutely aware of not wishing to offer 'tips for teachers'. However, there is nothing within these pages that I have not either used in my teaching or observed in other classrooms. The next section of this Introduction considers the frameworks within which education is bound.

Who controls our teaching?

One of my great concerns for teaching, as a potentially fantastic profession, is the ever-increasing impact politics has upon what happens in schools and individual classrooms. At worst, the result is to reduce the teacher's role to that of technician, turning flair and creativity into a teaching-to-the-test mode. One sadness I have of this approach is the adherence or, at worst, a 'compliance' (how objectionable I find this particular word within education settings) to a political agenda which seeks to reduce children's learning and their achievements to simplistic 'measurable' outcomes. Sadly this agenda is dressed up in the clothes of 'standards' which, in turn, requires quantifiable data to provide information for publication in the form of league tables. Such reductionist forces may find favour in a Gradgrindian (*Hard Times*, Charles Dickens) philosophy: however, it leaves this twenty-first century citizen despairing over its limitations and its inadequacy. Phew, I feel better for that little rant! I believe we have to find ways of educating those who are likely to have little idea of the dynamics of life in classrooms or about what teaching entails. We must find ways of informing political and civil servants of the complexity of imposing structures and 'standards' in education in ways which fail to recognize that classrooms are emotional places; learning cannot be reduced to a series of levels or grades monitored by outside agencies.

There are a whole range of external issues that impact upon teaching, such as testing, targets, tracking, percentage of A to C GCSE grades achieved, inspection and so on. Some of these I only touch upon. The reason is that this book is more about teachers' central sphere of influence, what we are constantly capable of making an impression upon – our classroom and the students who come through the door. We cannot, however, ignore the impact that national policy has upon schools, departments and individual classrooms, and the next section in this Introduction looks at some of the pressures on mathematics teachers, particularly with regard to what has happened in education since 1989. I begin however just one year after 1984.

1985

In 1985, the seminal work *Mathematics from 5 to 16*, written by HMI, was published. It listed the aims for teaching mathematics:

- Mathematics as an essential element of communication.
- Mathematics as a powerful tool.
- Appreciation of relationships within mathematics.
- Awareness of the fascination of mathematics.
- Imagination, initiative and flexibility of mind in mathematics.
- Working in a systematic way.
- Working independently.
- Working cooperatively.
- In-depth study in mathematics.
- Pupils' confidence in their mathematical abilities.

I believe these aims are fundamental to the way we plan and carry out mathematics teaching, and this book is based upon trying to achieve them. There are always dangers of a list such as this being nothing more than a wish list, a set of platitudes that seem great in the form of policy, but difficult to transpose into practice. For this reason I have written a new chapter titled 'Strategies for implementing HMI aims in "Mathematics from 5 to 16" aims'. I also explore the kind of pressures mathematics teachers continually face from various quarters, particularly within a climate of testing and league tables.

6

Children are expected to meet so-called clear targets rather than work on mathematics in which sometimes a destination may be ambiguous or unclear. Under such conditions the main emphasis in teaching mathematics falls upon what can be tested, rather than assessing what is desirable to be learnt. Yet the list of aims produced by HMI in 1985 are *the* most important ideas, providing pedagogically-sound foundations upon which schemes of work can be based. Narrow testing, however, leaves such skills in the position of being hostages to fortune.

Assessment is inextricably linked to effective teaching and learning, and when wider forms of formative and summative assessment are encouraged, teachers can become confident to work in more creative ways. Teachers' professionalism must be recognized and this can be achieved through the responsibility they, and students, are given for assessing achievement. Fortunately the 'Assessment *for* Learning' agenda is becoming recognized as a potentially powerful way of supporting students' learning, and I develop this in the chapter: 'Daring to be different'.

Some concerns I have had about writing this book

While writing this book I have encountered a number of concerns, and I would like to take this opportunity to raise these, in order to share my awareness of the pressures practitioners face when teaching mathematics to groups of adolescents – the seemingly impossible task of 'getting the buggers to add up'. Having taught in schools from 1971 to 1995, I have gathered some experiences that I feel are worth sharing. I hope others feel they are worth reading about! From 1986 until 1995 I led a mathematics department where we taught across the 11 to 16 age range, entirely in mixed-ability groups. I also began to develop ways of teaching mathematics that did not use a textbook or any published scheme. Since 1995 I have worked full-time in teacher education.

My first concern, therefore, is that I am writing primarily for current and future practitioners who regularly teach mathematics to students going through rapidly changing physical and emotional states. I only occasionally teach within this age range now and while I continue to work with teachers in classrooms, my current teaching is mainly to older people.

My second concern is about prescription. Throughout this book I offer a wide number of ideas based upon practice. Of course, many of these will already be in use in many classrooms: others, however, may be relatively new or currently unused and may have potential for being incorporated into schemes of work undergoing development. I am conscious, however, that any idea is only as good as the intention behind the person wanting to use it. I do not, therefore, seek to prescribe ways of teaching; and this leads me to my third concern. Anybody reading this book could easily think 'well, yes, in an ideal world ...'. However, nobody inhabits an ideal world. Utopia does not exist and it is certainly not worth waiting around for someone else – a head of department, a headteacher, an advisor, a politician, Bill Gates or God (unless he/she is IBM compatible) – to change things for us. There is only one person who can create change in my classroom and that is me.

I sought to create my version of an ideal world by teaching in mixed-ability groups, without textbooks and mostly using problem-solving, equipment-based approaches. Of course, I have worked with students who have exhibited difficult behavioural characteristics, and certain students have caused me a lot of concern. There have been times when I wished I could turn the clock back and take back something I'd said or say something I hadn't said. On the whole, however, the children I taught were great and there were hundreds of occasions when amusement and laughter occurred simultaneously with the learning of mathematics. Students would often enter my classroom with smiles and hellos and leave the room with 'See you next lesson'; these were not rare events. Occurrences such as these form the fundamental basis of what makes teaching so fantastic, so worthwhile.

This takes me to my fourth concern, namely the title of this book. *Getting the Buggers to Add Up*, as a title for a book, may well appear to be putting labels not only on the children but also on notions of what mathematics is. I have pondered this concern for some time, and the opportunity to write this book strongly outweighs any concerns I might have about its title. This is because I believe I have something to contribute to the wider debate on teaching and learning mathematics ... I stopped being in the bottom stream a long time ago! The word 'buggers' does not refer to a particular section or group of children. I often use it as a generic term: indeed, it is a word I frequently use when a small mishap occurs, such as forgetting to pack the coffee in my rucksack (Bugger!), or when I become impatient for my computer to start up (Come on you bugger). Likewise, mathematics is clearly much more than merely adding things up; again, I hope not too many people will take strong exception to the use of the image of 'adding up' as a wider description of learning mathematics.

Getting the Buggers to Add Up therefore is my attempt to offer alternative visions and different ways of teaching mathematics. For some, the book may serve to strengthen and consolidate their beliefs about teaching mathematics; others may have different, more adverse reactions. One or two politicians or civil servants may dip into the book and consider the policies that drive the teaching of mathematics and think 'I wonder if these tests really are driving down standards ...'. Whosoever reads this book, I hope there is something within the pages that will have some small impact upon pedagogy.

Pedagogy: fantasies, reality, contradictions and rationalization

To complete this Introduction I debate the issue relating to the external assessment structures that are placed on schools and offer thoughts about rationalizing the contradiction between learning mathematics and examining mathematics.

Two fantasies

To begin, I invite readers to briefly enter into a fantasy world, based upon the question: 'Suppose all the syllabi and curricular and textbooks in the school disappeared?' This is taken from

Teaching as a subversive activity by Neil Postman and Charles Weingartner, and is followed by: 'Suppose all of the standardized tests – city-wide, state-wide and national were lost. In other words, suppose that the common material impeding innovation in the schools simply did not exist. Then suppose that you decided to turn this "catastrophe" into an opportunity to increase the relevance of schools. What would you do?' (1971, 65)

I have always found this a fascinating and thought-provoking question. To consider visiting such a fantasy world, even briefly, where tests do not drive the curriculum and textbooks and schemes do not pervade mathematics classrooms is worth exploring. This is because by seeking to answer Postman and Weingartner's question I am thrown onto my own resources and encouraged and challenged to decide just what I want to do in my mathematics classroom and how I would want to do it. The question is a catalyst to consider pedagogy, my what, my why and my how that underpin my teaching rationale.

Here is another fantasy: suppose there was a government imposed 'rule' where nobody was allowed to spend more than two weeks of mathematics lesson time in direct preparation for the tests? (There would of course have to be test-sniffers to monitor this rule, somebody like an Oftest inspector to check out how long schools were spending on test preparation; anyone found to be doing more than two weeks worth of such activity would be publicly named and shamed!) Given this scenario is unlikely to come to fruition, I believe it is worth asking: what is the absolute minimum amount of time we need to use to focus on test preparation? Minimizing the focus on testing has implications for maximizing the time spent on 'real' learning and this has implications for how we plan our lessons, the resources we use and the strategies we implement. However, before getting carried away with such autonomous, free-spirited and anarchistic thinking, I must consider the reality.

Reality

The reality is that tests exist and schools are measured according to the grades students' 'achieve'. Just how far these grades reflect children's mathematical capabilities or how far they match the amount of time and energy put into test preparation are other issues. We might well wonder how we arrived at this situation, of schools being measured on a market-force, value-for-money and politically driven model. Within my experience the politicization of education began with the Callaghan 'Ruskin' lecture in 1976 where the 'secret garden' of education was opened up to scrutiny. The Thatcher/Major governments and the 'back to basics' movement gave rise to the National Curriculum in 1989. The Blair government spawned prescriptive national strategies and things have gone downhill from there (or upwards on a political spiral).

Successive governments have needed to show their policies are 'working' and to achieve this, simplistic measures, related to students achieving higher levels on national tests and grades at GCSE and A-level, have become the benchmarks. Pressure to increase test scores cascade down from central government to LEAs, from LEAs to headteachers, from some headteachers to departments, from some department heads to classroom teachers and finally from some teachers to children. Within our free-market economy publishers make a lot of money by selling texts to accommodate this preparation for the annual testing frenzy. A question still exists, however, about the amount of time teachers and students need to give over to the tests and, therefore, what is the absolute minimum amount of energy which needs to be spent preparing for them?

Contradictions

Sadly, all of this testing and the strive for the holy grail of improved levels and grades is contradictory; it is illusionary on one front and potentially damaging on another. The first relates to the relative value of the qualifications gained and whether there is any connection between scores on tests and mathematical capability or attainment. Year after year newspaper columnists comment upon standards. For example: 'Pupils who score 45 per cent on GCSE maths papers are getting A grades' (Warwick Mansell, *Times Educational Supplement*, 3 December

2004). Passing a test tells us little about other important qualities that teachers strive to enculture in students, such as becoming competent and caring individuals and learning the value of being responsible and rational people.

The second issue relates to the difference between students doing lots of revision to prepare for tests and students understanding mathematics and becoming more confident and capable mathematicians. The latter requires teachers and students to work together. Trying to find out what mathematics any individual student knows, really knows and understands, is a complex business. Trying to find out what a class of 30 or so individuals know is perhaps impossible. Well, this doesn't sound particularly positive; perhaps, therefore, it is worth considering some ways a teacher might be able to find out what students know. I develop this presently.

Rationalization

A fundamentally important issue for any teacher to engage with is to find the balance between achieving personal and professional autonomy, and resisting prescription emanating from top-down autocracy and overzealous bureaucracy. We can achieve the former by developing our pedagogy, by considering what we believe to be important and rationalizing how to teach effectively while at the same time revealing our values (I develop the issues of value-in-action in *Creating Positive Classrooms*, 2004). In the mathematics classroom I seek to achieve this aim by careful consideration of how I want students to experience mathematics. How I plan my teaching is 100 per cent focused on how I intend my students to experience learning.

First of all, my entire curriculum is grounded within enquiry, upon problem-posing and problem-solving approaches to learning and teaching. Second, I use a variety of strategies to encourage students to enquire into and engage with mathematics. Third, I use a range of resources to support students' mathematical concept development. Fourth, I try to ensure that assessment and recognition of students' achievements is multi-faceted; by which I mean I use different ways of assessing achievement, and each approach is integrated into teaching and learning. Finally, I seek to teach mathematics in two distinct ways. One is 'pure' mathematics where the structures and relations, the connections, the logic and the complexity of mathematics are explored, for example:

> *Find a data set which has a mode of 3, a median of 4 and a mean of 5.*

Another approach is a cross-curricular manner where students have opportunities to see how mathematics both models and helps to make sense of natural, physical, sociological and economic environments. A simple example of this would be to ask students to collect data from home such as:

> *Find out how many household tasks are carried out in a typical week at home.*

Students can then work on questions such as:

> - *How much time does each task take?*
> - *Who does them?*
> - *What proportion of the time taken for tasks done at home is carried out by different people?*
> - *How could this information be represented pictorially?*
> - *What are the implications of your findings?*
> - *Can data from different students' households be compared?*

Both of these ways of working are within the tradition of problem-posing and problem-solving and require me to find ways of reducing my didactic mode of teaching and increase the time I spend encouraging exploratory approaches to learning

Pedagogy

Developing problem-posing and problem-solving approaches to learning and teaching mathematics is a recurrent theme throughout this book, and as such it is worth asking what a problem-posing/problem-solving mathematics curriculum looks like. To begin to answer this question I find it useful to consider what such a curriculum would not look like. It would not look like students being asked to provide answers to decontextualized, 'shallow' questions, typical of the kind we can see in exercises within most and probably all textbooks. These are not what I consider 'problems' or problem situations. The over-use of textbooks is anti-educational on a number of fronts and this is because:

- they are trivial and fail to offer students' meaning;
- they do not deepen students' understanding;
- they fail to help students make sense of the interconnected nature of mathematics;
- they can occupy a great deal of students' time with little to show for their endeavours;
- they are boring both for students to do and for teachers to mark!

Typically, textbook questions are based upon practising a specific narrow skill, for example:

Round the following up to two places of decimal: a) 0.61532 b) 3.7891 c) 23.0237.

While some students will answer all of the exercise questions correctly, such an event does not help students understand *when* it is useful to round a result of a calculation to a certain degree of accuracy. Neither does this approach help students transfer what they have learnt to another situation (and frequently another lesson).

The examples below describe problem-posing and problem-solving approaches to learning and are taken first from an event in 2004 and second from an idea I have used many times in classrooms.

At the 2004 Association of Teachers of Mathematics (ATM) Easter conference I had the great pleasure of organizing two workshops with Keith Windsor about ideas for mathematics classrooms to cross the KS2 to KS3 'divide'. One mathematical problem was based upon finding three sets of values using the numbers from 1 to 9, so each set added to 15. Although delegates initially divided the values into three sets of three, Keith suggested there were other solutions based upon unequal sets of values, for example {9, 6} {8, 5, 2} and {7, 4, 3, 1}. This intervention opened the problem up and provided the group with a wider range of solutions to find.

A further problem during the same workshop was: how many ways are there of summing prime numbers to a total of 41? When planning this we knew there were at least four different solutions; what we had not bargained for was just how many more solutions existed. As the delegates found more and more solutions we found ourselves learning a great deal more about the value of working on such a seemingly 'simple' problem. Extending this problem by trying to prove that all possible solutions had been found was a further level of complexity and would certainly provide an opportunity to challenge students who have a range of different potential attainments.

A task I have used several times, usually with Year 7 students, and which is also written up in the ATM publication *Learning and teaching mathematics without a textbook*, is as follows: Take four squares and make some shapes by joining them full edge to full edge. What different perimeters can be made?

Now suppose we relax the rule and allow squares to touch both full edge to full edge and half edge to half edge, for example:

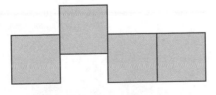

What different perimeters of shapes can now be found?

Suppose we relax the rule even further and allow joins at the corners as well?

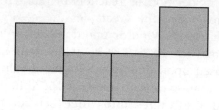

What range of perimeter values can now be found? Can all the perimeters be found from the minimum to the maximum going up in ½s? What about all the perimeter values going up in ¼s? How can I make perimeter values of 9.7 or 10.35 or 11.137?

The ideas I have suggested above are typical of the kind of ideas that appear throughout the book. How we develop our pedagogy is dependent both upon our determination to make learning interesting and upon the influences that colleagues and external stimuli offer. I was indeed fortunate enough to be strongly encouraged to develop problem-posing and problem-solving approaches to my teaching both by my first head of department, and then by my headteacher when I became a head of department myself. It is my hope that anyone who reads this book will feel encouraged to take risks, to try out new ideas but most of all to consider the impact of the ways we wish to teach upon those we have responsibility for teaching.

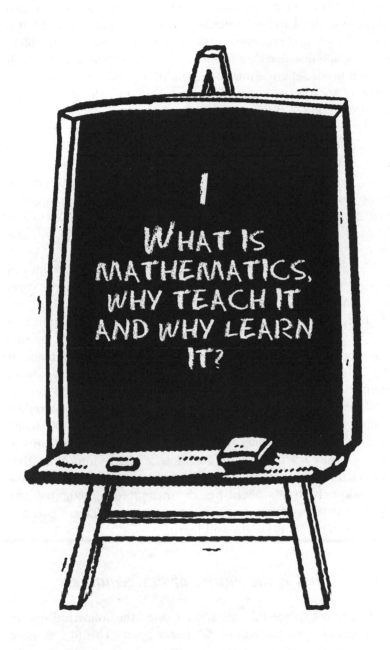

1

WHAT IS
MATHEMATICS,
WHY TEACH IT
AND WHY LEARN
IT?

Mathematics is beautiful, intriguing, elegant, logical, amazing and mind-blowing; a language and a set of systems and structures used to make sense of and describe the physical and natural world. It is a set of tools and processes used in decision-making, a discipline upon which questions are formulated and problems are solved. It is used to model environmental conditions and applied to make sense of social phenomena. Mathematics can help build bridges and bring food to the hungry.

Mathematics is frightening, boring, debilitating and can appear illogical; a thing many people made, or make, little sense of at school. It can be used to discriminate and separate children into those who can and those who cannot, those who do and those who do not understand and, as a consequence, mathematics can serve to undermine many individuals' confidence as learners. Mathematics can be used to create weapons of war and destroy the economic and social fabric of societies.

The degree to which an individual perceives mathematics in positive or negative ways will largely be determined by the ways mathematics is experienced at school and in the home. I believe all disciplines are of equal value: they are dependent upon one another and have an infinite number of meeting points. However, mathematics holds a particularly interesting place in the curriculum as *the* subject that creates barriers and causes learners a deal of stress and anxiety. It is important therefore, as teachers of mathematics, that we occasionally pause to reflect upon what we think mathematics is, ask ourselves why we teach mathematics and consider what experiences we want students to have as they learn mathematics. It is similarly important that politicians and educationalists, who have a key responsibility for the way children's learning is 'measured', recognize the significant impact that methods of assessment have upon the way mathematics is taught and learnt.

What is the nature of mathematics?

To begin to explore this question I offer the following quotes from sources written almost 50 years apart. The first is from

Richard Courant and Herbert Robbins in their 1941 book *What is Mathematics*:

Mathematics as an expression of the human mind reflects the active will, the contemplative reason, and the desire for aesthetic perfection. Its basic elements are logic and intuition, analysis and construction, generality and individuality.

The second is from 'Non-statutory Guidance', a National Curriculum Council publication from 1989:

Mathematics is not only taught because it is useful. It should be a source of delight and wonder, offering pupils intellectual excitement and an appreciation of its essential creativity.

Reflecting upon some of my own experiences as a learner, there was a lot of 'mechanical' arithmetic and I did plenty of exercises. However, I was not taught about the puzzlement of mathematics and neither was I taught to appreciate its creative or aesthetic value. I subsequently recognize that the value I now place upon education is related more to the *way* I was taught than *what* I was taught. In art lessons, for example, I was encouraged to make decisions and provided with choices about *how* to go about a task; this gave me a greater interest in learning than being 'made' to do countless exercises and pointless calculations, and to apply seemingly useless formulae. As a teacher of mathematics, therefore, I need to recognize how I responded to the way I was taught and consider how I might teach in order to provide students with access to the fascination of mathematics. This begs important questions about what I think the nature of mathematics is, why I teach mathematics and how I might encourage students to learn mathematics.

Seeking to understand the nature of mathematics is also a useful precursor to ways I deal with the kind of questions adolescents inevitably and quite understandably ask about why they need to learn mathematics. Trying to convince students about the value of learning trigonometry as a way of finding out where to stand when a tree falls down may provide some mirth:

however, is unlikely to provide many with a sufficiently convincing justification about why they need to learn it. Yet stopping to think about what the nature of mathematics is can be unnerving, challenging, complex and illuminating.

Considering whether mathematics exists as a set of rules that individuals from different civilizations throughout the centuries have 'discovered', or whether it is something that has been constructed and 'invented' as a means of describing the world, is a worthy area for discussion. Such questions can be posed to students and would sit comfortably in a mathematics classroom where exploration is encouraged or through curriculum initiatives such as 'Philosophy for Children' (P4C). As busy teachers, however, who have tomorrow's lessons to plan, marking to do and reports to write, entertaining such thoughts for more than a short period of time may be a luxury we feel we can rarely afford. Yet if our engagement with such ideas underpins what we do in mathematics classrooms and impacts in fundamental ways on how we teach mathematics, it is important to dwell upon such questions.

Because I see mathematics as a language for describing and giving meaning to natural and social phenomena, this impacts upon how I work with students in mathematics classrooms. Because I see mathematics as a set of tools or ways of thinking in order to solve problems, I use problem-solving as a significant methodology in helping students learn mathematics. I see mathematics as a set of interrelated systems and structures, connected in many different ways: therefore a key aspect of my role is helping students to see such links, to learn to connect ideas together, as well as making sense of concepts themselves. Because I see value in helping students make personal meaning and sense of what mathematics is, in my teaching I encourage students to ask difficult questions about what mathematics is and what the purposes and reasons might be for them learning mathematics.

So – why learn mathematics?

Some of the more debilitating questions students might ask any teacher are: 'Why are we doing this?'; 'What's the point of learning all this stuff?'; 'What use will this be to me when I leave school?' Such questions might be construed as fairly confrontational, especially if the teacher perceives they are asked in a particularly surly manner or that a student's timing has been 'inch-perfect' in terms of stopping the teacher when in full flow! Students are intelligent enough to realize that questions such as these provide good sport for testing out the teacher, or at least are a potential distraction from the lesson. On the other hand, such questions, perhaps asked in a more positive manner, might be a student's genuine desire to understand something, to go deeper into the mathematics. Whatever the reason, once a question has been posed it can be very difficult to ignore and seemingly impossible to answer in a way that is likely to placate the questioner. Instead, however, of seeking to offer glib answers to such questions, I intend to consider what a mathematics teacher might do to use such questions in a positive way and prevent them from turning a lesson into a difficult experience.

Pre-empting the inevitable and valuing openness

Something I frequently find both interesting and useful is to ask a whole class a question such as: 'What do *you* think the point of learning mathematics is?' Sometimes I ask this kind of question at the beginning of a new academic year, often arranging the chairs in a ring (*circle time*) and initially asking pairs of students to discuss this question for a minute or two before taking any responses. Such a question can be posed to all ages of students ... sometimes I get more coherent responses from 11-year-olds than from undergraduates! Sometimes I ask such a question while a class is working on a particular topic. On other occasions it is posed as a homework task, to be picked up and discussed in the following lesson. The important issue is to ask students what they think is the value of learning mathematics. My intention is

21

to create an atmosphere of trust and openness where students' views are valued and where I invite students to scrutinize, interrogate and evaluate mathematics. This may sound incredibly highfalutin and theoretical, yet, having taught thousands of adolescents, I find this approach particularly valuable. This is because it is a planned aspect of practice, designed to challenge students to question the value of mathematics for themselves.

Bugger – this is beginning to read like 'tips for teachers', something I wish to avoid in this book. The 'big' issue is about the value of determining the kinds of attitudes and atmospheres we want in our classrooms. The beliefs we hold determine what 'goes on' in our classrooms and how our students experience and make sense of mathematics. Examining our beliefs and deciding how we want the culture of our classrooms to be, look, sound and feel, are personal decisions we choose or choose not to make.

The remainder of this chapter focuses on ways I try to apply the issues raised above to school mathematics, and on methods of engaging children in mathematics in the classroom.

How do we learn mathematics?

What does it mean to learn mathematics? I ask this question because I have a concern that the strong emphasis in recent years upon testing, league tables and inspection has inevitably drawn teachers' attention, understandably so, to how to enable more students to pass more tests, for the percentage of A to C at GCSE to increase, for their school to climb ever higher up the league tables and for more lessons to be considered of a higher quality than ever before. Remember the washing powder advert that promised to wash clothes even whiter? Sometimes it seems education is measured along the same kind of lines . . . if only life were so simple! Yet do all our efforts at teaching, to gain better results, to achieve higher positions in league tables and to get better marks from inspectors equate to 'better' learning?

Before thinking any further about what learning mathematics means it is worth considering what learning anything means, and I invite you to consider the following questions:

- What was the latest thing you learnt?
- Why did you choose or why did you need to learn it?
- How did you know you had learnt it?
- How will this learning help you in the future?

These are not easy questions to answer. This is because learning rarely happens in bite-size chunks or in specific moments we can readily identify; when we gained some knowledge which we have internalized, understood and can to transfer to another situation. I can recall certain events, such as learning to fix a puncture, use a compass, drive a car, cook a curry and the words of 'You'll never walk alone'. (This was belted out wonderfully at the Liverpool v. Chelsea Champions League semifinal at Anfield – and what a night that was.) However, how I learnt skills of analysis, to analyse a film or a text, how I learnt to wordprocess and how I learnt to prove certain geometric 'truths' are much more complex affairs. I cannot easily determine how 'good' I am at carrying out such complex and often abstract concepts; so it is with mathematics.

For example, learning how all the concepts involved in graphing a quadratic function are connected together requires a depth of study. Understanding how ideas of crossing points on the x-axis (if any exist), the crossing point on the y-axis, the turning point, the line of symmetry, factorization, completing the square algorithm, the impact of changing the coefficient of the x^2 term, etc. is complex. To cause students to make sense of all this information I need to a set up a number of interconnected learning experiences. I must find ways of helping them explore and discuss quadratics, turning points, crossing points, etc.; above all I must help students process all this information. Giving students a formula to help them regurgitate the solutions to a quadratic equation may help them answer a question in an examination, but what have they learnt? Providing a correct or a desired response to a narrow question in a short period of time in a high-stakes examination is not going to create the environment for deep learning. One of the more disturbing things students may have learnt, however, is mathematics is a load of gobbledegook.

This in fact was what an A-level mathematics student told me a couple of years ago. This event took place when I was helping a neighbour to prepare for his AS mathematics examination. He was a diligent and highly capable student and we spent a couple of evenings going through past papers. Towards the end of the second evening he turned to me and said: 'I hate maths, Mike!' His comment was neither intended nor received as a sign of his thanklessness for my help, it was a cry from the heart. He could jump through all the necessary hoops and he would go on to gain a grade A in the AS examination, yet he had little or no idea of the fundamental processes he needed to apply. Although this is but one anecdote about one highly capable mathematics student being turned off mathematics, his story resonates with the kind of concerns raised by Professor Adrian Smith's enquiry into post-14 mathematics education, *Making mathematics count* (2004). In a letter to the Secretary of State for Education, in the Foreword to the report, Smith wrote: '. . . we have a curriculum and qualifications framework that fails to meet the mathematical requirement of learners, fails to meet the needs and expectations of higher education and employers and fails to motivate and encourage sufficient numbers of young people to continue with the study of mathematics post-16.' This must be something of a concern to everyone involved in mathematics education, especially as there are so many recurring themes and concerns raised 22 years prior in the Cockcroft report.

Throughout this book, therefore, I seek to offer visions of approaches to teaching mathematics (based upon my reality) that will provide students with positive learning opportunities, which will respect students' integrity and will seek to build on what students *can do* as learners of mathematics.

Learning mathematics is about constructing new knowledge and here the role of the teacher is crucial in terms of how the learner is helped to formulate their constructions. When knowledge is used and applied in problem-solving situations, concepts become assimilated into learners' existing knowledge base. The issue of skills emerging though problem-solving resonates with a quote from the Cockcroft report: 'Mathematics lessons in secondary schools are often not about anything. You

24

collect like terms or learn the laws of indices with no perception of why anyone needs to do such things. There is excessive preoccupation with a sequence of skills and quite inadequate opportunity to see the skills emerging from the solution of problems' (1982, para. 462). Learning mathematics, therefore, is a mixture of conscious and unconscious competence, of students knowing instinctively how to make sense of a problem, and of being prepared, and have the confidence, to work hard on something when 'stuckness' stares them in the face.

Accelerated learning? How about deepening and decelerating learning instead?

I have become increasingly concerned over the use of ideas such as Accelerated Learning. My concern lies with the notion of students being rushed to engage with mathematical concepts at too early an age. There are dangers of students being accelerated to get to the end of a mathematical journey at the expense of enjoying and making sense of the views on the way. To quote Robert Pirsig from *Zen and the Art of Motorcycle Maintenance*: 'To live only for some future goal is shallow. It's the sides of the mountain which sustain life, not the top' (1974, 199). A consequence of accelerated learning is that students miss out on the pleasure of seeing wider aspects of a mathematical journey in order to arrive somewhere at a faster rate than might be good for their deep conceptual development. I also have concerns about students being encouraged to end up at a predetermined place and once they arrive there being sent off an another journey which might bear little resemblance to their previous route.

As an example I offer teaching Pythagoras' theorem to 13 or 14-year-olds, where the outcome of their learning is for them to recognize the connection between the areas of the squares drawn on the sides of a right-angled triangle. There is, however, so much more to explore and speeding students on to something else causes them to miss out on other vital pieces of knowledge. For example, suppose other similar shapes are drawn on the sides of right-angled triangles, such as equilateral triangles, pentagons, hexagons, semicircles or even similar-shaped rabbits? Suppose the original triangle is not right-angled (i.e. triangles which have one obtuse and two acute angles or triangles which consist of three acute angles)? One way to test students understanding of Pythagoras is to give them problems which require the application of Pythagoras' theorem to reach a solution, yet the problem itself does not immediately say 'use Pythagoras'!

For example:

> *On a 16-dot (4-by-4 grid) draw a scalene triangle with the largest possible perimeter. What does it look like?*

Because the solution is a non right-angled triangle then using and applying Pythagoras' theorem may not be immediately obvious. This means some students will have to dig into their mathematical toolkits and make consciously competent decisions to use the tool of Pythagoras to reach a solution. Other, perhaps more intuitive students, will automatically use Pythagoras' theorem without so much as a pause. There will be other students who may not know where to start, in which case there is even less point in trying to accelerate them off onto something else.

Whatever the scenario, the central issue is the need to help students construct new knowledge and to deepen their understanding from the basis of whatever their existing knowledge is. To achieve this students need to be provided with problems to solve that are initially accessible and ultimately challenging. They must be provided with opportunities to be actively involved in learning mathematics. Of greatest importance, they must be able to gain a sense of achievement about how, as well as what, they learn.

Learning mathematics through problem-posing and problem-solving

An approach I frequently use in order to encourage students to engage with mathematics is to pose a problem. Through problems I seek to:

1. Provide access to students in terms of everyone being able to offer some kind of answer.
2. Gain a variety of answers or encourage different ways of working on an idea.
3. Help students move towards an understanding of a specific concept.
4. Cause students to work on ever-more complex areas of mathematics.

I refer to this list as my planning criteria. Using it helps me to determine the kind of strategies I might employ at the beginning of a lesson and starting points I can use for a sequence of lessons.

A simple example might be to pose a question, say to a Year 7 class, such as:

> *In how many different ways can I multiply two whole numbers together to make 42?*

In relation to the planning criteria, this question:

1. Can be made accessible.
2. Has a variety of answers (1×42, 2×21, 3×14, 6×7).
3. Might be used to explore divisors of numbers as the specific concept, using 42 as an initial example.
4. Opens up the possibility of exploring other concepts such as developing ideas of prime factors, working with non-integer values, and engaging with the square root of a number.

Throughout the planning process I need to maintain a sense of *what* I intend students to learn and how this fits into long-term plans described in a scheme of work. This may, or may not match prescribed, non-statutory, national frameworks. My short-term planning together with moment-by-moment interactions in lessons will determine *how* I teach and, therefore, *how* my students experience mathematics. Moment-by-moment interactions are not things I can plan for; I can only raise my awareness that they will happen and work on my ability to respond to events in positive ways in order to accommodate the unexpected. I can also celebrate that this is what teaching, in problem-posing, problem-solving ways is largely about, and it cannot be predetermined or prescribed. An example of how I can plan for or intend my teaching to impact upon students' learning within a problem-solving pedagogy is to ask them to consider what they think they are learning. This process – of helping students become explicit about their learning – is important if I am to aid them in making sense of mathematics and see what the wider picture looks like.

Mathematics and creativity

Sadly, mathematics is not widely thought of as a creative discipline. Yet when creative mathematical thinking is encouraged, when questions open up different possibilities, students have opportunities to see for themselves that mathematics can be creative and not limited to right or wrong answers. In such circumstances students grow to believe they are capable of finding more than one answer to a problem or that there may be more than one way of carrying out a task. Consequently, students feel they have something to contribute, something worth saying. There are important principles here about enabling a wider range of students to participate in whole-class discussion; this requires the use of a far wider range of strategies than the commonly used 'hands-up' approach. To achieve this participation, greater use can be made of open questions. A challenge is how to take a closed question such as 'What is 7 add 3?' and turn this into a more open question.

Asking open questions

There is a plethora of questions and problems that can open up the possibility of students offering different answers and methods. How answers are accepted and what value is given to answers received are key aspects of practice based on asking open questions. A simple example would be a question such as:

> **How many different pairs of whole numbers can I add together to give an answer of 10?**

This provides students with the possibility of offering several answers. If in my planning I choose to develop this question, to encourage the use of fractional, decimal or negative values, there are an infinite number of answers to the original question and this is another valuable idea for students to engage with.

If students subsequently turn some of the pairs of values that add together to make 10 into coordinate pairs, they can see how answers can be represented as a graph. The focus could be shifted to naming this graph, with the intention that some students begin to feel comfortable with the equation $x + y = 10$. However, because we cannot expect all students to make such a conceptual leap, we might ask those students who do understand to explain to those who do not. This is a valuable strategy, momentarily turning some students into 'teachers' and, by explaining what they know to someone else, deepening their knowledge of the concept. The original question could be changed to: 'Find some pairs of numbers that add up to a total of 8', and by graphing these students will have an opportunity to recognize that this graph is parallel to the earlier one.

The initial question can be tweaked so it becomes:

> **Find pairs of numbers that multiply together to make 12.**

Graphing these results will produce a different picture, and this is connected to the earlier '42' problem. To develop students' thinking we might ask what happens if one of the two numbers is 5, thus causing student to work with decimals and see that the values (5, 2.4) also fit onto the graph. Sorting out the equation $y = 12/x$ raises further complexities. All the time, developments can be suggested by altering some aspect of the original question. How we deal with the inevitable fact that some students will understand ideas faster and to a greater depth is all part of the differentiated learning that exists in all classrooms. The challenge is to find teaching strategies to accommodate different learning outcomes.

The beauty of the planning process lies in being able to apply it to many kinds of problems to provide students with access to all areas of the mathematics curriculum. This process is developmental, in terms of students working on ideas that underpin and extend conceptual understanding.

Ideas offered so far in this chapter have been of a type where the starter question can lead students into different, though connected, concepts of the mathematics curriculum. I now consider working the other way round: deciding upon a broader concept and considering how I might provide all students with access to a particular concept. I use Pythagoras' theorem as an example.

A problem-solving approach for teaching Pythagoras

In planning to teach Pythagoras we might ask ourselves questions such as:

- What is Pythagoras' theorem essentially about?
- What other concepts are linked to Pythagoras' theorem?
- What kinds of puzzle or problem might I pose to provide students with access to, and the opportunity to construct, an understanding of Pythagoras?
- What strategies might I use to cause students to practise and consolidate their understanding of Pythagoras' theorem?
- What kind of development or enrichment ideas might I use to extend students' thinking?

The last three questions match planning criteria 1), 3) and 4) in the earlier list and, therefore, the planning framework is similar. The spider diagram opposite is an attempt to explore some of the concepts that underpin and are linked to Pythagoras' theorem. As it stands there is much missing, such as taking a historical perspective to consider how the concept we know as Pythagoras' has roots in Egyptian, Babylonian, Chinese and Indian cultures. The issue of proving Pythagoras is another substantial area for consideration. Neither have I included the idea of drawing semi-circles on the sides of right-angled triangles, or indeed any similar shape. Each of these can provide useful extension work, and I develop such ideas later.

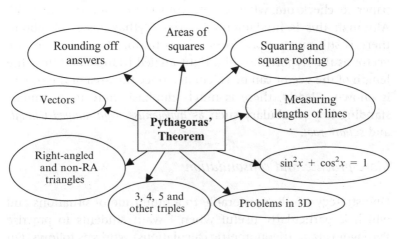

Having begun to explore the terrain, I need to decide what starting-point problem I might pose to help students construct an understanding of the theorem. My personal favourite is to provide students with pegs and pegboards, so each person has ten or a dozen pegs of their chosen colour. The idea is to play a simple game called '*Four-in-a-square*'. Players take turns to place pegs in the board and the winner is the first person to place four pegs on the four corners of a square. Once a square has been made, students draw this on square grid paper and work out the following information from each square:

1. Write one side of the square using vector notation.
2. Calculate the area of the square.

As more 'slanted' squares emerge the information can be collected together and fed back to the whole class, perhaps by making an 'instant' display of lots of A4-size pieces of sugar paper, each with a vector and the area of the square written with a large marker pen. With 20 or so separate pieces of information around the room students can engage the BIG question: to try to connect together the elements of a vector with the area of the square.

Once students have begun to form an idea about what is happening, they can draw other 'slanted' squares on square grid paper to check out whether the conjecture continues to hold. Although this is fundamentally what Pythagoras is all about, there is still much work for students to do. This is to 'see' the vector as the hypotenuse of a right-angled triangle and how the length of the vector can be calculated once the area of the square is known. Clearly, there is much emphasis here upon understanding key vocabulary such as *hypotenuse, right-angled triangle* and *square root*.

More practice and consolidation

One strategy I find transferable to a multitude of situations and which is particularly useful when I want students to practise Pythagoras (and trigonometric calculations) works as follows. On 1-cm square grid paper (and eventually on plain paper), students draw some right-angled triangles, initially with the two shorter sides having integer length. They then apply Pythagoras' theorem to calculate the length of the hypotenuse. Having worked out this result to one decimal place, they measure (with a ruler) the length of the hypotenuse and check whether their calculated answer is the same as their measured result.

Students do as many of these as they need to, in order to consolidate their understanding of the procedure. (I develop issues of practise and consolidation in Chapter 13). There is an issue here about trusting students and creating a situation where they can take the initiative and the responsibility to do as many calculations as they feel is necessary. In my experience I find students who struggle with mathematics usually do many more examples than those who understand what the procedure is all about. This is one aspect of working with differentiated learning.

Furthermore, and because I would teach Year 7 students how to program a graphical calculator (see Chapter 9), older students have the skill base to write a program for Pythagoras' procedure. Once such a program has been written, students feed information in and speedily get information back. Again, here there is the issue of differentiated outcomes and the importance of providing students with sufficiently challenging tasks, based upon having and using the basic tools for solving problems.

Extension tasks

Beyond working out the length of one of the short sides of a right-angled triangle, a further task is to explore what happens when squares are drawn on the sides of non right-angled triangles. This is intended to lead students to construct inequalities $a^2 + b^2 > c^2$ and $a^2 + b^2 < c^2$, depending upon whether the triangle has all acute angles or has one obtuse angle.

There are plenty of other problems and developments for students to work on, such as:

- Exploring what happens when semi-circles (or any similar shapes) are drawn on the sides of a right-angled triangle.
- Working out the distance between any two points (x_1, y_1) and (x_2, y_2)
- Finding out the length of the 3D diagonal in a cuboid.
- Finding different sets of Pythagorean triples.
- Connecting Pythagoras with $\sin^2 x + \cos^2 x = 1$.
- Proving the result. There are very many proofs, yet the important issue is that students are encouraged to try and construct a proof themselves.

Using and applying Pythagoras' theorem

The most difficult issue for students in using and applying any mathematical skill or concept is being able to recognize, as discussed on p. 26, what tool they can pull out of their mathematical tool kit to help solve a problem. If students come to rely on their teacher to suggest which tool they might need to use, there exists the possibility that students will not be able to think for themselves. If, however, students are brought up in a problem-solving environment, where they are encouraged to become independent problem solvers, they are better equipped to decide what mathematics they might bring to a less obvious situation. The following problem, originally offered to me by Liz Meenan of Channel 4, opens up such a possibility and makes use of old packs of cards kindly donated by my local Bridge Club.

1. Take a playing card.
2. Fold the top left-hand corner onto the bottom right-hand corner.
3. Fold the two 'triangular' bits over so that you have something that is almost, though not quite, an equilateral triangle. These will become 'flaps' (see figure below).

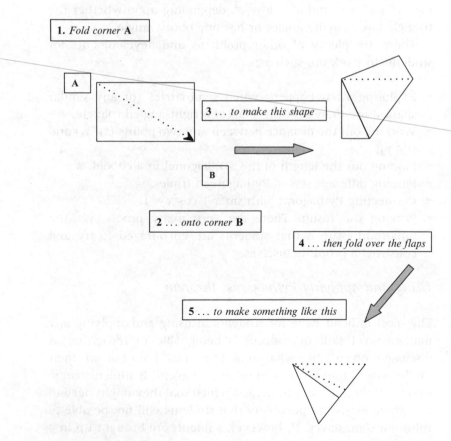

1. *Fold corner* **A**

A

3 *... to make this shape*

B

2 *... onto corner* **B**

4 *... then fold over the flaps*

5 *... to make something like this*

4. Now take a second playing card and fold it the opposite way to the first one (i.e. fold the bottom-left corner to the top-right corner).
5. Repeat step 3.
6. Unfold the two cards.
7. Now put them together to form a tetrahedron (with 'flaps' on the 'outside').

The problem is as follows:

> **If the solid were a <u>regular</u> tetrahedron, what dimensions would the playing card have?**

Solving this problem requires students to:

- recognize the need to use Pythagoras' theorem;
- manipulate surds;
- apply Pythagoras in a non-obvious context.

Once students have sorted this out they can take a pair of scissors to the cards and snip away. Interestingly enough, we only have to snip two or three millimetres off both long sides of a playing card to create a rectangle close enough to produce the required size. I mention this to make the task accessible to students who might be too young to conceptualize Pythagoras but who can still have an opportunity to experience this tetrahedron-making process.

Even further developments

If we fold four such cards each time the 'same' way these can be formed into an octahedron. This requires rather deft handiwork and having two pairs of hands may prove useful.

Now, because a tetrahedron and an octahedron tessellate in 3D space, there is an opportunity to challenge the most confident of school-aged mathematicians to calculate the dihedral angles of the two solids and prove why they fill 3D space.

Alternatively, if we are interested in a visual impact, we can stick one tetrahedron onto each face of the octahedron and be amazed at the outcome, a compound of two (intersecting) tetrahedra. This process can be continued as more octahedra fit into the 'holes' created by the last group of eight tetrahedra: then more tetrahedra will fit into the next set of 'holes'. What happens when more tetrahedra and octahedra are added is something I am still working on. I have an intuition about the eventual formation of a large octahedron at some point in this growth process ... I have just not got there yet.

'Good' mathematical tasks that stand the test of time

The process I have gone through in this chapter – considering what mathematics is, why and how I seek to teach mathematics and how I want students to experience mathematics – has implications for planning and determining the strategies and tasks I might use. Over recent years, mathematics teaching has become ever more prescribed in terms of curriculum, levels and targets; this prescription has been backed by testing regimes. More recently, mathematics teachers have been given greater guidance nationally about how the prescribed curriculum 'should' be taught. As such, it becomes increasingly difficult for teachers to prioritize time to create their constructions of what mathematics is and decide for themselves how everything fits together. Yet because there is no one way to describe mathematics or one method for teaching mathematics it is important to make such decisions for ourselves.

One thought has remained with me consistently throughout all the changes and curriculum iterations. If I have an interesting mathematical idea, or a useful way of providing students with access to mathematics, this will hold good, in my classroom, whatever the curriculum looks like and whoever is directing proceedings. In order to be confident that the ideas we have are valuable and will stand the test of time, it is important to go in deep and ask the searching question: *What is mathematics?*

2

STRATEGIES FOR TEACHING MATHEMATICS

In this chapter I consider the kinds of strategies at teachers' disposal for use in classrooms. Having a range of ways of teaching clearly supports students as there are different ways of learning. At this juncture, however, I am conscious of not wishing to jump on the preferred learning styles/visual, auditory, kinaesthetic (VAK) bandwagon. This is because I am troubled by the notion that each individual has a specific or a dominant learning style that can be determined. In reality, students respond to a variety of stimuli; this means providing a planned, eclectic approach to teaching to create powerful learning opportunities. Furthermore, even if we could 'objectively' determine what the preferred learning styles are for different individuals, I am not sure what any teacher does with such information. For example, when I walk into a classroom I can take for granted, with a 100 per cent certainty, that there will be a range of students who have different levels of understanding, different approaches to learning, different amounts of food in their stomachs and will be in different emotional states. OK, so if I know this, what do I do with this information about levels and preferred learning styles for each of the 25 to 30 students present? How do I use such information to plan a lesson and how do I begin to teach the lesson? Recognizing that different individuals will learn at different rates and understand ideas to different depths indicates I need to employ, over time, a range of different teaching approaches. It is, therefore, my responsibility to use a range of different strategies, resources and stimuli to accommodate such differences. In order to provide a context to discuss different strategies I refer again to the seminal publication by the DES, *Mathematics from 5 to 16* (DES 1985).

Although much has happened in mathematics education in the 20 years since DES 5–16 was published, little has changed in terms of the underpinning philosophy upon which mathematics is most effectively taught and learnt. Indeed, this publication is, I believe, the philosophical bedrock upon which the various National Curriculum iterations and National Strategies are based. What is important and valuable about DES 5–16 is the way this underpinning philosophy is captured in ten listed aims and discussed and disseminated to practitioners in less than 15 double-sided A4 pages.

In this chapter, therefore, I discuss some of the issues coordinators, heads of department and individual teachers may wish to consider if the all-important DES 5–16 aims are to be brought to fruition. It would be superficial, however, to suggest each aim can be mapped onto specific strategies or particular ideas for use in the classroom. Nonetheless, it is valuable to provide examples of how these aims might be achieved in order to shift thinking about learning and teaching from policy to practice and from rhetoric to reality. Because the first five aims are about aspects and perceptions of mathematics and the second five are about ways of working in a mathematics classroom, I have only focused on the first five aims in this chapter. Before going further, however, I offer the following quotes from Ofsted mathematics subject reports: the first was published in 2004 and the second in 2005:

> For pupils to use their mathematical knowledge and skills to solve problems in different contexts, they need secure conceptual understanding. In the best lessons, teachers deploy a range of teaching strategies, pupil groupings and types of task to enable pupils to develop a secure understanding of the ideas being taught...

> Classroom tasks challenge pupils to think and reason mathematically.

Both of these quotes emphasize the importance of problem-solving through different approaches and the value of offering challenging tasks; I build on these ideas below.

Mathematics as an essential element of communication

Mathematics might be considered a tool of communication in the following ways:

1. As a language containing its own specialized vocabulary.
2. As a shorthand requiring communicators to understand signs and symbols.

As such, students need to learn the vocabulary, read the signs and understand the symbols. The specific vocabulary of mathematics is clearly substantial. Trying to write as many 'mathematical' words beginning with the letter 'a' in, say, two minutes is an interesting activity and can of course be turned into a 'Boggle' type game for use in the classroom. Perhaps you might want to try such an activity for the next couple of minutes before reading further. Here's my list (no peeping until you've done yours): area, arc, angle, algebra, algorithm, apex, altitude ... time up ... how many did you write? To make sense of vocabulary there needs to be hundreds of in-context opportunities where vocabulary is strategically and explicitly used. Here are five strategies I have used:

1. Write any mathematical words on the board which arise (or which I strategically decide to bring to students' attention) as a lesson progresses ask students to copy these down. There could be a possible homework task here by asking students to write a definition of each word, or to give them the task of explaining the list of words to someone at home.
2. Ask students to construct a personal mathematical dictionary using loose-leaf A5 paper.
3. Ask students to write the definition of a word, perhaps with a picture to illustrate their meaning, and to put such information on sugar paper for display purposes.
4. This fourth strategy was something I regularly employed and was based upon writing a precis, or a record, of how a topic had developed over a two, three or four-week period on large sheets of sugar paper using big felt markers. I would list the starting point of the development tasks and any specific vocabulary as the work developed. This meant a class had a visual *aide-memoire* of the ongoing work and I had a place to keep a record of key words.

v) Asking students to write about the work they are doing or have done is a regular feature within the domain of GCSE coursework. However, students need to learn and develop the skills of how to write about mathematics from an early age. When a student can explain a mathematical process, in writing, such as Pythagoras' theorem, how to find the volume of a solid or how to calculate a 'missing' side in a right-angled triangle, they deepen their understanding of the concept. Concepts of Pythagoras, volume and trigonometry are in the domain of KS3 and KS4 students, yet this issue is just as, if not more, important at a younger age. So, for example, for a KS2 student to do only half as many multiplication calculations and to then explain their understanding of what multiplication means would be time well spent.

Learning how to communicate mathematical understanding and to become explicit about implicit knowledge is, therefore, central to mathematical concept development.

Mathematics as a powerful tool

For students to appreciate mathematics as a powerful tool they need to be presented with problems to work on so they can see how mathematics is used to reach solutions. There are two distinct ways mathematics may be viewed in this context.

The first is as a set of systems, structures and relations, which are underpinned by logical and abstract thinking. The ultimate power lies in the power of constructing a proof; I have frequently heard professional colleagues, usually at ATM conferences, refer to an 'elegant' proof. I have also heard my undergraduates jokingly (I hope) put their heads in their hands and exclaim in mock exasperation (again I hope), 'Oh no, not the dreaded "P" word again!' This phrase came about during a geometry module I had the pleasure to teach, or should I say the fun of repeatedly asking '... but can you prove it?'

Typical problems involving proof were:

- angle/circle theorems;
- proving why there are only five Platonic solids;
- folding a flat knot in a strip of paper then proving the resulting shape is a regular pentagon;
- proving the centroid of a triangle is ⅓ of the distance between each vertex and the mid-point of the opposite side.

Regarding school mathematics, the challenge is to present problems so students can seek to create a proof of the solutions they produce. For example:

- proving they have found all the possible triangles on a 9-pin square geoboard;
- proving Pythagoras' theorem;
- proving the outcome of the '1089' problem (see page 63).

The second aspect of appreciating the power of mathematics relates to real, 'real-life' problems. There are any amount of these which require students to use or develop modeling skills. I am conscious, however, of the dangers of creating pseudo contexts; those contexts which provide an 'excuse' for doing mathematics ... such as the builder who uses formulae to determine how many different coloured paving flags are needed to build a patio. I develop this issue in greater depth in Chapter 8, 'Teaching mathematics through "real-life" contexts'. Real, real-life contexts impact directly on children's and adolescents' lives. For example, the recent, and timely, attention 'healthy eating' has received opens up marvellous opportunities for students to engage in the mathematics of food and energy. Through mathematics students can make sense of the calories we need to provide us with our energy requirement, the kind of exercise that burns up calories and the fat content of different foods. Exploring average daily calorific input on the one hand and exercise on the other and looking at ways of producing mathematical models to explain these can also open up cross-curricular opportunities. Similarly, exploring issues of smoking, perhaps carrying out a 'truth' survey and using data collected from the whole school, will provide enormous opportunities for students to work on the mathematics of health-related issues. I have written about this particular idea, as a cross-curricular theme, in *Creating Positive Classrooms* (2004).

Appreciation of relationships within mathematics

Mathematics is fundamentally about appreciating and understanding relationships, for example:

- between the lengths of the sides in a right-angled triangle;
- between angles through circle theorems;
- between the Fibonacci sequence and the Golden Ratio;
- between height and circumference of head;
- between coordinates and vectors;
- between a quadratic function and the turning point of its graph.

Creating opportunities for students to form connections between mathematical concepts is clearly important in terms of deepening their confidence and competence with mathematics.

A further key issue is for students to perceive mathematics as an interconnected set of skills and concepts and to help them recognize how and where such connections exist. One useful strategy is to encourage students to draw spider diagrams showing how the key mathematical concepts they are currently working on connect with previous work they have done. For example, a module of work which has a central focus on measuring, perhaps producing a scale diagram of a classroom or various areas of the school or of the students themselves, can lend itself to different 'subordinate' skills being learnt, used or developed. Some of these skills are:

- rounding to an appropriate degree of accuracy;
- scale factors and drawing to scale;
- interpreting answers from a calculator;
- calculating perimeter;
- calculating area;
- units of measure.

One idea to utilize some of these skills is to designate different areas of the school to pairs of students. One student calculates the average length of one 'ordinary' pace (say by measuring ten paces and finding the average) then paces out their plot or area. The other person keeps records of the number of paces on a rough outline of the area being paced out. Upon returning to the classroom, each pair uses this information to produce a scale diagram of the area measured out. Of course, if all information is to make any sense then an agreed scale, say 1 to 10, would be necessary. Extension ideas could be to calculate the perimeter of different buildings and the acreage of certain areas or playing fields. For students to know there are 4,840 square yards to an acre will provide them with plenty to think about when working with metric measures.

At the end of the module a whole-class discussion about what skills they have been using and considering where they have met any of these previously in mathematics lessons is a valuable strategy as part of the sense-making and the interconnectedness agenda.

Awareness of the fascination of mathematics and Imagination, initiative and flexibility of mind in mathematics

I have put these two together because they seem to me to be so closely connected. For students to become fascinated by mathematics, this places a substantial responsibility upon teachers to provide potentially fascinating ideas for students to explore. The *source of delight and wonder* quote from the 1989 Non-Statutory Guidance (p. 19) fits perfectly with this aim; seeking to achieve it is what makes teaching mathematics such an interesting and intriguing challenge. I cannot emphasize enough the value of puzzlement as a strategy to fascinate students, to cause them to use their imagination and be prepared to work in flexible ways. The other week I came up with an idea I have never actually used in an 11–14 classroom, and what I was interested in was how such a simple idea could be used to work on students' puzzlement factor. Take one brightly coloured piece of A4 paper (preferably giving a class different colours to make the resulting display attractive). Ask them to make two folds in their paper which intersect and so neither are parallel to the edges of the paper. The problem is to find the minimum number of angles that have to be measured so all the 12 angles can be worked out. Alternatively, students can be asked to measure one of the angles at the intersection between the two fold lines and one of the angles where a line meets the edge and use this information to calculate all the other ten angles.

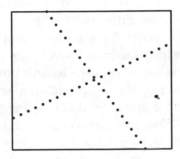

An extension task is to label one angle (at the 'centre') α and one angle (at the edge) β and then to write the size of every other angle in terms of α and β.

The task can be developed in two different ways to challenge students. One is to fold/draw a line perpendicular to one of the two initial lines so a triangle is created in the middle of the sheet. The second is to fold/draw three lines so two are parallel and the third passes through both lines. With these situations it is possible to create 24 or 20 angles and, as before, the same questions can be posed. A key issue here is for students to recognize how angles can be determined from a minimum amount of information ... and again, not a textbook in sight!

Here is an anecdote about a lesson I had the privilege to observe in January 2005. The purpose of the lesson was to revise for a test.

Revision class

The students are revising for a science test which they will be doing the following week. The teacher has asked a boy to come to the front of the classroom with his exercise book and use this to make up and ask questions about the work the students have done. The boy quietly asks a number of questions and as each question is read out members of the class eagerly wave their hands in the air wanting to be the one to answer the question. The boy points to one of his classmates, an answer is received and the boy moves on to ask his next question.

Next, a diminutive girl comes to the front – I can barely see her face, partly because she is so small and partly because her exercise book, which she proudly holds up is partially covering her face. Her voice, however, booms out as she asks her questions. As before, the other children strive to be chosen; some are almost out of their desks in their enthusiasm to provide answers. The little girl seems as if she is imbued with assertiveness through making the choices about who is to answer each question; she points to her classmates in a determined, careful manner. The teacher, meanwhile, appears on the surface not to be doing anything.

This is a shining illustration of a teacher being able to 'take a back seat' because she has already done all the hard work of teaching by:

- instilling a sense of responsibility in her children;
- utilizing a teaching strategy where students are temporarily invited to play the role of (another) teacher;
- creating a positive relationship with the class;
- demonstrating that learning is not just 'fun', it is significantly important.

The above anecdote occurred on a bright sunny morning in January 2005 in a class of 7- and 8-year-old children. The school is situated on the outskirts of Asmara, Eritrea. There were 42 children in the class. I know this because there were 21 small bench-type desks in the room; two years ago, a colleague reliably informed me, in the same class there were three children to each bench. The only visible resource was a blackboard with a scratched surface and some sticks of white chalk. Because the lesson was conducted in Tigrinyan, I could not understand a word of what the children were saying, however, the school director (headteacher) explained what was happening; my earlier analysis of the strategies the class teacher employed is, therefore, my subjective interpretation. However, it was not too difficult to see enthusiastic and motivated children and observe a seemingly relaxed and skilled teacher at work. This is an example of what I consider an excellent teaching strategy, where the students are actively engaged in their learning and are taking responsibility for their learning.

In the following four chapters about surprises, people-math, using practical equipment and approaches to mental mathematics, I offer further examples of the kinds of strategies that are at any teacher's disposal. However, before moving on to Chapter 3, I have a concern relating to the strategy of writing one's objectives, which I discuss below.

The orthodoxy of objectives

Many years ago I saw a cartoon in a newspaper which had a person dressed in medieval clothes sitting on a rock in the pose of 'The Thinker'. A thought bubble read: 'I think ... therefore I am a subversive.'

The notion of teachers writing lesson objectives on the board has, over the past few years, become a new received orthodoxy; in some schools, I hear of senior staff and heads of department spending valuable time checking that classroom teachers are compliant in carrying out this new orthodoxy. This checking procedure is also on the agendas of Ofsted and local authority inspectors (advisors). Children, it seems, are no longer to be 'left in the dark' about their teacher's intentions; transparency rules and learning follows directly from teaching ... just as night follows day ... if only life in classrooms was quite so simple!

I think it is vitally important for teachers to discuss with a class all kinds of issues relating to learning such as:

47

- the approaches a teacher believes are important to support students' learning;
- helping students understand the value of what they are learning;
- the value of students engaging in their learning in positive and responsible ways.

I also believe it is important to discuss last night's score at the local football game (especially the wonderful night at Anfield when Liverpool beat Juventus 2–1), or about the latest band to 'hit the scene'. However, how and when I choose to engage in such conversation is down to my professional judgement.

Likewise, whether I choose to share with a class what I intend 'us' to work on and to try to make sense of is a professional decision I intend to be in a position to make. I do not want other people who occasionally pop into my classroom, and therefore cannot begin to understand the nature of the relationships I am developing with a class, to determine my teaching behaviours for me. In order to deconstruct the value of writing specific, narrow learning objectives I raise four concerns and discuss each of these below. They are:

- teacher autonomy and professional judgement;
- differentiated learning and continuation lessons;
- student responsibility;
- surprises and unpredictability, ambiguity and uncertainty.

Teacher autonomy and professional judgement

For any teacher to learn about teaching, they need to engage with issues of autonomy and autocracy. If all I had ever done, as a teacher, was what some higher, supposedly wiser, authority had told me to do, and this person had passed on prescribed methods and ways of working, then my teaching capability would have been severely limited. However, I was fortunate enough to have a first head of department, in my formative years of teaching, who encouraged autonomous and creative thinking. Of course there was a basic framework (scheme of work) and support mechanisms (including personal and curriculum development opportunities) in place, and I relied upon these to help me with my development. These provided a 'safety net', which was so important in helping me come to know myself as a teacher; to know how far I could extend my approaches to teaching and to decide when to play safe. I was also encouraged to try out a range of teaching strategies, to take 'risks' and to share what I was doing within the department; this created a culture of openness and trust. My first concern, therefore, about writing objectives on the board is of teachers doing so because they have been told to do so. This undermines autonomy and subverts professional judgement. Of course, if a teacher chooses to write objectives on the board because they firmly believe this is an important part of the learning process, because they have analysed and rationalized the reasons for doing so, this is another matter altogether. This is an example of a teacher making an autonomous professional judgement and this must be respected.

Differentiated learning and continuation lessons

Learning takes place at different speeds and to different depths of cognition for different people. As such, if I, as teacher, manipulate the learning (or the outcomes of learning) so all students achieve the same objective in a lesson, I must have moved the lesson along at too fast a pace for some *and* at too slow a pace for others. Teaching a 'one size fits all' pace will not benefit a class because there will be as many paces and depths of learning in a class as there are students present. For example, if I pose a problem such as 'try to find all the different nets of a cube', students will inevitably find the solutions by working at different paces and in different ways. I can see little value therefore in moving a whole class towards an answer that there are x amount of different nets if, by doing so, my intervention becomes an interference. I do not want to run the risk of mathematically interfering with some students' engagement in the task who are trying to find out this information for themselves, at a pace commensurate with their current level of cognition.

Of course I have a responsibility to deepen the mathematical experience of those students who quickly find all the solutions, and to do this I need to have other tasks, such as 'try to prove you have all the nets'. Other problems might be to explore which nets 'tile' the 2D plane, and this can lead students to explore which shapes might, in theory, be the best to minimize waste.

Taking students' differentiated learning (both speed and depth) into account meant many of the lessons I taught in secondary classrooms were continuation lessons. A new topic would be introduced in one lesson and continued over the following five, six or even ten lessons. How far different students developed their understanding of the central concepts within the topic varied considerably. Sustaining a topic over a period of two, three or four weeks meant students had opportunities to develop their thinking, explore ideas to different depths and learn one of the most important life skills of taking personal responsibility for their work. I develop this final point below. However, had I begun each lesson throughout a given period of time by writing an objective on the board (beyond 'develop the task you are working on') this would have served to fragment students' experiences of mathematics and reduce their learning to 'bite-size' pieces. The dangers of fragmenting mathematics into tiny pieces is something we can leave to many of the textbooks on the market; we don't have to subscribe to this style of teaching in order to fulfil a potentially ill thought-out approach to learning mathematics.

Student responsibility

The phrase 'students taking responsibility for their learning' is easy to roll off the tongue, yet a highly complex issue for teachers to help their students engage with. For students to recognize the importance of taking responsibility it requires them to create and inhabit a classroom culture that encourages autonomy and celebrates individualism. There is an important parallel here about teachers being similarly valued for their professional autonomy and, in turn, students similarly being encouraged to think for themselves. When students make autonomous, mathematical decisions they ultimately become more responsible learners. I believe this is one of the most important, yet most complex, aspects of life in a classroom; all the time I feel teaching is analogous with walking a tightrope, balancing what I want to happen in a classroom with what students are doing. If I am to educate my students to take responsibility, then I must also learn when to take a step back, when to loosen my grip and to trust that, over time, the vast majority of students will 'do the business'. All of this is complex and is connected to classroom culture, to my expectations of myself as a teacher and to individual students as learners. Expectation in a classroom must be a two-way process; just as it is important for the teacher to have high, yet realistic, expectations of their students, students also have expectations of how I, as their teacher, will support and encourage them in their learning as well as their social development.

A key aspect of student responsibility is connected to them setting their own goals, within a supportive, negotiated framework. Personal goal-setting is something which must arise naturally as a consequence of the work students do in terms of the developmental and exploratory nature of the work on offer. For example, if a student is finding all the different rectangles that can be made with areas of 20 cm^2 on 1-cm square grid paper, there exists a range of extension tasks. This means that as students engage with different degrees of complexity, the goals, in terms of mathematical understanding, change. What each student needs to understand is what the subsequent goals might be and to determine how far they are capable of developing the problem. For students to engage in extension ideas, the culture of the classroom must be based upon an understanding that there are always other ideas to explore and an expectation that students will develop their work as far as they can within the time available. Often it will be useful to negotiate with students how much more time they think they need, and this will often be determined by interest levels and whether a topic may be drying up.

If student responsibility, therefore, is to be taken 'seriously' it is not feasible for the teacher to take the responsibility of setting an objective because individuals in a class will inevitably have different goals to achieve, particularly, as described above, if a topic continues over a sequence of lessons.

Surprises and unpredictability, ambiguity and uncertainty

Finally, I am at a loss to understand how objective-setting can embrace surprises or countenance unpredictability. Deep learning occurs when students make sense of something they have had to puzzle out, something they have had to work hard on. Some students may have had cause to backtrack, to be systematic, to look for 'blips' in a set of data or try to make sense of unexpected outcomes. Mathematics holds very many surprises and here is one such example.

On the circumference of a circle draw two nodes and join them together with an arc. This arc splits the circle up into two regions. Now draw a circle with three nodes and join them with three arcs and we have a diagram with four regions. With four nodes we have six arcs and eight regions and with five nodes, ten arcs and 16 regions. With six nodes we do get 15 arcs but do *not* get 32 regions! (This assumes the 'rule' for joining nodes is no three arcs meet at a single point.) So, while the number of arcs conform to the triangular number sequence (1, 3, 6, 10, 15 . . .) the number of nodes does not conform to powers of two. A situation which appeared as though the sequence 2, 4, 8, 16, 32 . . . was emerging produces something quite different. The following chapter contains further surprises.

Mathematics is more than a list of content knowledge (Pythagoras, trigonometry, etc.) to be learnt in bite-size pieces. It is a beautiful, intriguing and mind-blowing subject which can encourage learners to engage in deep, independent and shared thinking. Through mathematics students can learn to take responsibility and engage in personal development, and develop their understanding at different paces and to different depths. Objective-setting when framed in a narrow sense of 'this is what you are going to learn' militates against ambiguity and uncertainty, and this is an important aspect of mathematics which students need to understand. On the other hand, students need to recognize there are an abundance of situations in mathematics where proof rules OK and where generality lies at its heart. The objective for today's lesson is to 'blow your mind!'

3

Mathematical Surprises

> ‘Surprise and the unexpected rank high in the fabric of mathematical fascination, whether originating in the nature of mathematics itself or in the remarkable relationships between its different branches or, more simply, in paradoxes and puzzles.’
>
> *W. J. Reichmann (1967)*

Things that surprise me make me to stop in my tracks, take a second and third look and analyse events or make sense of the phenomenon that has captured my attention. My analysis might be to extol the beauty of something, to proclaim an interest or to want to capture a memory of it and possibly share it with others. Walking one early morning in Scotland on New Year's Day 2002 produced several surprises. The first was to be setting out on the hills before 8.00 a.m., when many respectable folk may have been nursing a slight hangover. The second was to see snow-cast mountains to the west take on a pink hue, and a pale then piercingly bright yellow sun cover the landscape to the east. The third surprise was to attain the summit cairn by 10.00 a.m. But wait a moment – I am meant to be writing a book about teaching mathematics, so what is all this blathering about winter hill walking? The strong connection for me lies in seeing teaching mathematics as an extension of many things I do in life beyond the classroom. Walking the hills is about freedom, challenge, exploration, making decisions, using navigational skills, making and recovering from errors, being exhilarated, enjoying the simple things in life and opening myself up to surprises. All of these qualities and sensations are important aspects for me in the classroom and for me, mostly, within mathematics classrooms. Mathematics is rich in surprises, in 'Aha!' moments, in challenges and struggles, as well as providing many opportunities to grab students' attention.

Grabbing students' attention

While it would be absurd to suggest that every lesson needs to be some kind of performance, there are times when I want to have fun, to engage students with challenging problems and, at the same time, be the craziest person in the room. I want to keep them guessing as to whether or not I have fallen off my perch. To try to achieve this and to grab students' attention I work on the mystery, intrigue and the surprise of mathematics, both through the starting points I use and the way I offer them.

There is always the danger, however, that 'good' starting points may be seen merely as pleasant, entertaining, attention-grabbing devices intended to sustain students' interest over a short period of time. Yet in effective learning environments there is much more than the teacher providing starter tasks. What happens over subsequent lessons, when students are expected to develop a task or practise and consolidate their knowledge, is crucial to helping them grapple with and make sense of mathematics. Students also need to expect to have to work hard on a skill, to practise it and get better at it. This is no different to the pianist practising his scales or the athlete building up her fitness: both require hard work and dedication. The magic elixir I look for is how to create classroom environments where students are prepared to work over 'dead' times. This is so they see for themselves that practice, in order to get better at mathematics, to experience the pleasure that lies within the surprising world of mathematics, is worth doing.

Finding ways of grabbing students' attention by providing problems that hold surprises and at the same time offer challenges is fundamental to helping them engage with mathematics in ways that are neither boring nor predictable. There are many problems that provide surprises, and I now describe some of my favourites.

IRATical surprises

IRAT is my acronym for an Isosceles Right Angled Triangle. The problem involves an exploration of what happens when IRATs are folded 0, 1, 2, 3 and 4 times and each time cut down the line of symmetry.

I usually begin this problem by holding up an IRAT and asking everyone to write down some things they know about the shape, followed by asking individuals (though not using a 'hands up' approach) to say what they have written down. Quite quickly a list of the properties of the shape emerges. This list almost always includes its colour and the fact it is a piece of paper! All comments offered are gratefully accepted and written on the board. After a short time enough information is usually provided to describe the shape accurately, establish or remember its name and become explicit about its properties. Interestingly enough, the symmetry of the shape is rarely mentioned. In such circumstances I usually tell or remind students about this property. I take a pair of scissors to the shape and cut it along the line of symmetry to produce two *similar* IRATs, each one being half the area of the original. The diagram below illustrates this, with the dotted line being the line of symmetry along which the original triangle is cut.

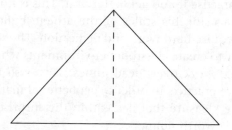

The problem develops as follows:

1. Fold a new IRAT in half down the line of symmetry. A triangle half the size of the original will be formed, which will have its own, 'new', line of symmetry. Now cut this shape in half through this new line of symmetry and see what happens. Before revealing the result students could be asked to visualize and describe what shapes are formed in terms of name and area. It might be appropriate to use this to discuss ideas of 'similarity' (between one of the smaller

triangles and the original) and 'congruence' (of the two smaller triangles). This provides an in-context opportunity to engage with vocabulary.

2. With one fold and a cut, a square of area $\frac{1}{2}$ and two smaller IRATs of area $\frac{1}{4}$ are formed. At this juncture the students could be asked to find all the different shapes (and prove they have found them all) by joining the pieces together using the rule of same length of edges together. As an extension task, and if students know something about surds, they could be asked to work out the perimeter of each shape they make.

3. Now start again with a new IRAT and make two folds, each one along the line of symmetry. Cut the shape in half and see what happens.

4. The surprising result is as follows:
   After 0 folds and a cut, 2 shapes are formed.
   After 1 fold and a cut, 3 shapes are formed.
   After 2 folds and a cut, 4 shapes are formed.
   After 3 folds and a cut …

As suggested, this problem opens up several possibilities:

- Visualization and discussion about what happens (particularly after one fold and a cut and two folds and a cut).
- Using vocabulary such as similarity, congruence, equivalence, names of shapes, conservation of area, perimeter, and surds.
- Making shapes and working with simple fractions.
- Adding fractions to check that all the pieces from each 'experiment' total 1.
- Developing ideas of equivalent fractions. (This idea will emerge more readily if all the fold lines are drawn in, so IRATs from increasing numbers of folds will contain halves, quarters, eighths, sixteenths etc. respectively.)
- Trying to predict, in terms of the number and the sizes of pieces, what happens with greater numbers of folds.
- Writing the sizes of the pieces formed as decimal values.
- Writing the sizes of the pieces formed as percentages of the whole.

Moving the focus of attention to the sizes of the pieces provides an in-context task for comparing fractions, decimals and percentages. There is an important issue here about the pieces arising from the IRAT problem providing a 'real' context (i.e. the shapes are real and have been produced and used by students) with which to work on ideas of fractions, decimals and percentages. This is very different to the typical kinds of exercises found in textbooks, where students are often asked to provide answers to closed problems without rhyme or reason (I develop this in Chapter 12).

Because the 'sequence' of the number of shapes develops 2, 3, 4, 6, 9 ... there is much for students to explore and sort out. All the time, possibilities exist for exploring fractions with denominators of powers of 2. Trying to predict how the sequence develops is in itself a sizeable challenge and will provide the most confident students with something to think about; indeed, having such challenges ready, to offer as extension tasks, is the basis for working with differentiated learning. The idea will certainly be a challenge for most 14 and 15-year-old students.

The next idea is intended to help students develop concepts of negative powers of 2 acting as the denominator of fractions.

An opportunity to grapple with the meaning of 2^{-1}

The denominators gained from the smallest triangle formed as each IRAT is successively folded and cut are halves, quarters, eighths, etc. After three folds we have sixteenths or ($\frac{1}{2} \times \frac{1}{2} \times \frac{1}{2} \times \frac{1}{2}$), which can be written as $\frac{1}{2^4}$.

By working this sequence of sizes of triangles backwards from $\frac{1}{2^4}$ to the original IRAT we gain the following information:

Smallest fraction	Denominator
$\dfrac{1}{16}$	$\dfrac{1}{2^4}$
$\dfrac{1}{8}$	$\dfrac{1}{2^3}$

$$\frac{1}{4} \qquad\qquad \frac{1}{2^2}$$

$$\frac{1}{2} \qquad\qquad \frac{1}{2^1}$$

Continuing this pattern the following results can be gained:

$$\frac{1}{1} \qquad\qquad \frac{1}{2^0}$$

This is the original IRAT of area 1.
The next result is:

$$\frac{1}{\frac{1}{2}\ \frac{1}{2}} \qquad\qquad \frac{1}{2^{-1}}$$

This must be two of the original IRATs added together which must, therefore, have an area of 2. Although this does not prove that $\frac{1}{2}_{-1}$ is equal to 2, it does provide a robust visual aid to help demonstrate it. What I particularly like about this demonstration is being able to 'show' for all to see a piece of paper that has an area of $\frac{1}{2}_{-1}$. Being able to demonstrate any abstract concept in some kind of concrete way is useful. Looking for opportunities to help students make sense of underlying mathematical principles is also one of the great joys and challenges of teaching mathematics.

Conservation of area and working with surds

The richness of any problem is measured by the variety of mathematical concepts that students can work on. Before leaving the IRAT problem, therefore, I offer a challenge that could be given to students who have some knowledge of Pythagoras. The task involves working with surds and calculating the perimeter of shapes re-formed from the pieces produced after folding and cutting IRATs.

Given the original triangle has edge lengths 2, $\sqrt{2}$ and $\sqrt{2}$ (in order to have an area of 1), the perimeter of the parallelogram formed by these two half-size triangles is $P = 2 + 2\sqrt{2}$. The perimeter of the square, formed by joining the resulting pieces from no folds and one cut, is $P = 4$.

The problem develops by making all possible shapes created from the three pieces formed from one fold and one cut and joined by equal length of edge. These are:

- one parallelogram;
- one isosceles trapezium;
- one rectangle;
- one asymmetrical pentagon;
- one symmetrical hexagon;
- two asymmetrical hexagons.

As before, the perimeter of each shape can be calculated: for example, the perimeter of the parallelogram below is also $P = 2 + 2\sqrt{2}$.

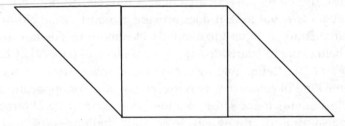

I can also ask students to produce a method to find all the possible shapes, which involves students engaging with fundamental aspects of mathematics, exploration and proof.

The IRAT problem is therefore packed with rich potential and can be used in various ways to support learning. I would choose to revisit IRAT on several occasions, depending upon the concepts I want students to work on. Making such choices is fundamentally important with regard to long-term planning and writing departmental schemes of work (I return to this in Chapter 10).

Given the intriguing nature of this problem, I should perhaps not have been surprised when on one occasion I found a colleague in the mathematics department – also a deputy head of school – who had used the problem each day of a particular week for assembly material ... Well bugger me! If you read this you know who you are!

A rich source of surprise resides within problems of a three-dimensional nature, and this is the focus of the next section.

A 3D surprise

Working on three-dimensional mathematics opens up further possibility for practical work (this is a focus in Chapter 5). Here I suggest a task that offers students a surprising result and can be used to help them make sense of an abstract concept. The idea is based upon making square-based pyramids; one outcome of this work is to demonstrate that the volume of the pyramid is one third of the volume of a cube into which it fits.

The problem can be given in different ways according to students' existing knowledge. The first version would be appropriate for students who have previously worked with Pythagoras' theorem and who have some experience of working in 3D mathematics, such as drawing nets and making solids. Under such circumstances I offer the following problem statement:

> *Make a square-based pyramid with side length and perpendicular height 15cm and with the apex perpendicular to one corner of the base.*

Depending upon the age and mathematical experience, other versions I might offer are:

1. Give students the dimensions of the pyramid but not a picture of the net.
2. Provide students with a scale drawing of the net and ask them to produce this on sugar paper using the dimensions suggested above.
3. Give students the shapes of the faces as templates and ask them to design a net.
4. Give students the completed net to cut out and assemble.

How simple or complex a teacher decides to make this problem will depend upon all kinds of circumstances and contexts that vary for different classrooms. Mathematically, the fourth of these tasks may seem to lack challenge. However, the outcome of the task is certainly something I would want all students to experience within a scheme of work and I must take into consideration students who have wide-ranging aptitudes.

When the pyramids have been made, I usually ask if I can 'borrow' three models and hinge pairs of edges together using sellotape. All three pyramids now fold up to form a cube. While this does not prove the formula for the volume of a pyramid, it is a useful demonstration to help explain why the $\frac{1}{3}$ appears in the formula. How this visual aid might be used to develop students' knowledge of volume of pyramids with any given dimensions is a key aspect of the task, and I am aware here of the autonomy of the teacher. I wish to make my own decisions about how to use an idea; the different ways I respond to students' questions will be determined by all kinds of knowledge I have about those I teach. Of course, there will be numerous occasions when I make decisions 'on the hoof' which I cannot plan for or predict in advance; this is what makes teaching such a fantastic job and underpins our professionality. I just have to keep remembering the slogan 'Don't let the buggers grind us down!'. I am not referring to students here.

Another 3D surprise

This idea is very similar to the previous one, although possibly more surprising, and certainly provides an amazing result. The problem statement I work with is:

> *Make a square-based pyramid so the apex is perpendicular to the centre of the base with side length x and a perpendicular height of $\frac{1}{2}$ x.*

As above, I can offer the same four alternative versions. Ideally I want students to make a lot of these, although once they have worked out the required dimensions for one solid they can use this as a template to make others more speedily. By joining six of these together, in the shape of the net of a cube (of which there are 11 different possibilities), a most interesting outcome occurs. This is that the six pyramids fold up into a cube: however, the surprise of this particular problem is yet to unfold ... literally!

By unfolding the six pyramids and wrapping the six square faces around another congruent cube, a rhombic dodecahedron is produced. Even more amazing is that a rhombic dodecahedron tessellates 3D space ... this could lead to an exploration of which other solids similarly tessellate.

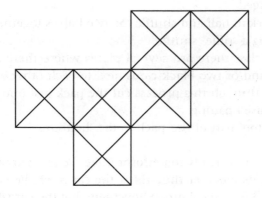

I have used the nets of these pyramids as a context for students to practise trigonometric calculations by calculating the angles of the triangular faces for each net. A more complex problem is to try to calculate the dihedral or the 'solid' angles of each pyramid. This problem will provide the strongest mathematicians with something of a challenge.

Other potential surprises

Writing a three digit number, reversing the digits, finding the difference, reversing this answer and adding it to the result from the earlier subtraction to produce the result 1089 has the potential to create surprise. This surprise might be enhanced if the teacher happens to have 1089 stuck on his or her back and at some point 'carelessly' turns around to reveal the 'answer' to the class.

Putting a banana in the filing cabinet prior to a class entering the room and holding a conversation about the probability of different events happening. At some point, asking what the probability is of finding a banana in the filing cabinet may cause a surprise ... it can also cause some amusement.

Finally, given the amount of enjoyment and surprise that can accrue from the use of playing cards and, in particular, carrying out occasional card tricks, I offer the following.

- Arrange a pack of cards red, black, red, black etc. throughout the whole pack and show students this is how the cards have been arranged.
- Cut the pack in half and shuffle the two halves together (once only), using a 'riffle' shuffle.
- Show the class there are several places where there are two red cards and/or two black cards next to each other.
- As you go through this process cut the pack just once at any same-coloured pairing.
- Place the 'top' part of the pack to the 'bottom'.

The 'trick' is now ready to perform. Take the top two cards and ask the students whether they think the cards will be both red, both black or different colours. Show them that they are different colours. At this point I tend to throw this pair of cards into the air with flair and gay abandon. Taking the next pair of cards I ask the same question – again they will be different in colour ... so will the next pair, the next, the next and indeed every pair. At some point in this flurry of activity I turn the cards over to reveal there are still pairs of red and pairs of black cards next to each other. Yet once the cards are turned over, followed by the utterance of some 'magic' words or by theatrically tapping the remaining cards, the trick continues; as each pair is removed from the top of the pack there is always one red and one black or one black and one red. By throwing the cards around the room and generally having a good laugh the showmanship side of my teaching style also emerges.

Well, this is definitely not magic! But it is mathematical and the challenge for students is to work out why the trick works.

Even without fully understanding why it does, students can carry out the process themselves, perhaps as a homework task to try out on someone; this might provide parents and guardians some insight into the kind of things that go on in mathematics lessons ... 'Well it was never like this when I was at school ...'.

Of course, surprises and a teacher's inclination to incorporate them into lessons, the way a teacher presents mathematical ideas, and the fun they seek to have is all part of the culture of the classroom. What is important to this teacher is to look for opportunities to have fun, to create surprises and to actively demonstrate that enjoyment is a key feature of learning.

There exist many other surprises to present to students, but if *beauty is in the eye of the beholder* then *surprises are in the eyes of the surprised.* Of course we can never guarantee anything, especially in classrooms. However, we can choose to work on creating opportunities for surprises to occur and, therefore, provide students with mathematical experiences from which they can gain *pleasure* and engage in the *puzzlement* and the *power* of mathematics ... the 3 Ps.

Intrigue and mystery

I remember a former colleague who frequently used intrigue as a powerful technique for gaining and holding students' attention. He suggested that taking a cardboard box into a lesson and pulling out the most mundane objects creates a sense of intrigue and stimulates students' natural instincts to want to know ... I have had enormous fun at times using the same strategy and it always seems to 'work' ... it's a mystery.

Creating a sense of mystery is probably the opposite of declaring one's objectives at the beginning of a lesson – well we are all different and, as an Eritrean teacher once told me: 'Differences are normal.' Imagine, however, the converse, where teaching is conducted in ways that are wholly predictable, so all we need do is complete the official three-part lesson planning form, follow the script, use the OHTs, download the PowerPoint slides and give out the prescribed homework at the end of the lesson. Thank goodness teachers are valued for autonomy, responsibility and professionalism.

Meanwhile, back at the cardboard box, instead of the soap box, a situation I always use with groups to create a sense of intrigue and fun occurs when I set up the 'painted cube' problem. This is a well-used problem and is described in many publications. As a class enters the room I surreptitiously say to one student: 'The answer to the question I shall ask you is "it's a bucket"'. To the next student I would say, 'The answer to the question I shall ask you is "it's quick-drying paint"', and to the third student, 'The answer to the question I shall ask you is "it's red"'. When the class are all assembled I hold up the cardboard box and ask the first student: 'What is this?', to the second I ask: 'What is in this bucket?' and to the third: 'What is the colour of the paint in this bucket?'. After each 'correct' answer has been provided I produce a white $3 \times 3 \times 3$ cube made from 27 linking cubes. I drop it into the cardboard box and pull out a red $3 \times 3 \times 3$ cube. Corny I know, but this always seems to captivate students and acts as a useful precursor to the problem to be worked on. What never fails to amuse me and, I guarantee, always happens, is some time later in the lesson when I 'casually' leave the cardboard box on the side, some student looks inside and says something such as 'I knew there was another cube in the box!'.

What I have described is about using intrigue as a strategy, as an element of my teaching style, to try to focus students' attention on a task. Mathematics, of course, holds many of its own mysteries and can provide students with much to think about. Some mysteries might be:

- Why the angle bisectors of a triangle meet at a common point.
- Why the side bisectors of a triangle meet at another, different, point to the angle bisectors (unless the triangle is equilateral).
- Why, when successive terms of the Fibonacci sequence are divided into one another, the answer settles out to 1.618 ... or 0.618 (depending upon which way round the divisions are carried out).
- Why a tetrahedron and an octahedron tessellate in 3D space.

- Why folding a strip of paper into a 'flat' knot produces a regular pentagon.
- Why the circumference of a circle is always three and a bit times the length of the diameter.
- Why ...

All these mysteries have explanations and seeking to cause students to figure out *why* certain outcomes occur are dependent upon providing problems for students to investigate. Developing students' thinking skills is fundamental to deepening their understanding of mathematics, and I develop this in Chapter 11.

Another of my favourite 'mysteries' is based upon the following problem.

- Take a strip of paper, say with a length of A4 paper and label the ends **A** and **B**.
- Make a fold line fairly close to end **A**.
- On this fold line write the number **1**.
- Now I ask students to enter into a 'pretence' that the distance from end **A** to the fold line marked **1** is ⅓ of the length of the whole strip.

The argument develops as follows:

- If this length is ⅓ of the whole, the remaining length from fold **1** to end **B** is ⅔ of the whole strip, and if I fold the distance between **1** and **B** in half I once again have a length ⅓ of the whole strip.
- On this fold write the number **2**

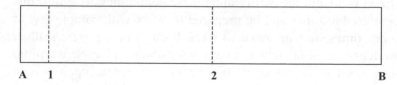

A   1   2   B

The distance from **2** to **B** is now a better approximation to ⅓ than the distance from **1** to **A**. By folding the distance between **A** and **2** in half, to gain fold **3**, we gain an even better approximation to ⅓. By continuing this folding sequence, to gain just a few more folds, something interesting happens; the seventh fold is virtually the same as the fifth fold and the eighth fold will coincide (visually) with fold number 6.

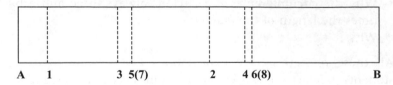

A   1   3   5(7)   2   4 6(8)   B

The mathematical explanation is that an iterative function, based upon the bisection method, is taking place; as the number of folds increases the approximation to $\frac{1}{3}$ gets closer. While this will not be a mystery to anyone who has worked on the problem, it can certainly appear mysterious to those who have not.

Using a similar method to produce a fifth, a seventh and any fraction with a prime denominator is a worthy challenge, particularly as the solution to this problems is so beautifully logical.

Teacher, performer, actor or just being oneself

At the beginning of this chapter, I mentioned the dangers of students coming to expect some kind of performance from their teacher. If students' contributions to lessons are largely dependent upon their teacher's performance, the downside is all too obvious. Teachers exhibit to various degrees in the art of performance and some will act in ways intended to create fun and laughter. However, learning mathematics also requires students to engage with difficulties, sometimes to enter uncomfortable zones and be prepared to work with complexity; at other times students need to work hard at practising a skill. If students are ultimately to take responsibility for their learning, they need to recognize their teachers as honest, open people with strengths and frailties, excitements and disappointments. Students need to recognize that their teachers work hard to support their learning, but cannot do the learning for them.

There are important issues here about discussing what learning mathematics involves and what this requires of students in order to be 'successful' learners. I would not wish, therefore, to give an impression that teaching is largely an all-singing, all-dancing performance: yet there are times when I choose to exhibit larger than life ways of being. This however is not an act; the way I teach reflects who I am. In whatever ways teaching is described, one of the crucial aspects of interacting with a class is to grab students' attention, to create a sufficiently interesting learning environment, to encourage students to engage with learning, and occasionally to give the buggers a surprise.

4

PEOPLE-
MATH

There are many problems that involve students getting out of their seats, leaving their desks and carrying out tasks in active, communal ways. This might appear to be a high-risk strategy, particularly if students are not used to working in such ways: as such, the ideas in this chapter need to be read with a sanity/ health warning, and treated with care. Setting up people-math tasks depends upon several factors. These include:

1. The value a teacher ascribes to active lessons and active learning.
2. The relationship a teacher has with a class.
3. The reasons, from a mathematical perspective, why such tasks might be utilized.
4. The reasons, from a generic learning perspective, to use such tasks.
5. The size of the room.
6. The teacher's energy levels.
7. Whether you have the support of another adult (for example, a Learning Support Assistant or a trainee teacher).
8. Whether the lesson is being observed.

With regard to 1), the values we take with us into the classroom have a massive impact upon how we teach, the resources and strategies we choose to use and the ways we respond to those we teach. In considering 2), I argue that using such people-math tasks can enhance teacher–student relationships. Of course, the converse can also be argued: however, I do not see the use of people-math ideas as a whether or not argument, I see it as a discussion about *why* and a decision about *when*.

I develop issues pertaining to 3) in the remainder of this chapter. Finding ways of tapping into different modes of teaching is the issue raised by 4). This is important if we acknowledge the different ways learning happens. Using different approaches in the classroom to vary how students experience mathematics is central to the issue of tapping into their different intelligences. Much has been written about this, particularly through the work of Howard Gardner on multiple intelligences (see Moon and Shelton-Mayes, 1994).

Room size is clearly something that has an impact upon a wide range of options: if the usual room is too small or if there are fixtures, such as benches, this may create difficulties. However, one thing that teachers are good at is making things happen and overcoming difficulties. If working on a people-math activity is seen as important, one might swap rooms with a colleague, utilize the school hall or go outside. With 6) in mind, we cannot of course legislate for how we might feel. Neither can we predict the weather or the 'way' a class appears when they enter the room. We can only adapt ourselves to circumstances; again, this is something at which we build up high levels of skills. With regard to 7), utilizing the presence of another adult can have many benefits, particularly when working in highly active ways. Finally, when considering 8), I strongly advocate the use of any of the tasks described in this chapter, whether in the presence of an inspector or another person who is observing a lesson; I speak from many first-hand experiences of being observed.

Sitting in a ring of chairs and giving everyone a number

There are very many tasks that fall under the title of 'people-math'. Below are some I have used, almost always with great success and much fun (many others can be found in Alan Bloomfield's book *People Maths*). As a consequence, students have engaged with mathematics in active and sociable ways. One furniture arrangement is to place chairs in a ring and desks around the edge of the room. This means that once the activity has come to an end, students can turn their chairs around and work at the desks; one outcome of this is that for the remainder of the lesson students face the wall; a different, if not interesting arrangement. Prioritizing the time required to rearrange furniture relates to the importance I place upon offering students people-math experiences. This relates to my pedagogy; I feel it is important to exploit different ways of supporting students' learning . . . *everything is connected*.

An interesting phenomenon I have observed on many

occasions relates to the reluctance of some students to sit next to someone of the opposite sex! Often, when students see the furniture in a ring, they arrange themselves in an arc of boys, a space, an arc of girls and another space! Before long, however, and as a consequence of the task they engage in, students lose their inhibitions about who they find themselves sitting next to.

Calculate my number

Once we are all sitting in a ring I randomly distribute integers, from one to the number of people in the room. I ask students to keep their number a 'secret', and make up some calculations, the answers to which will be their allocated number. One strategy is to ask students to use two or three-stage calculations, and, depending upon my knowledge or expectations of a class, I can suggest the use of brackets, powers, factorals, fractions, and so on. The intention here is for students to read out a calculation and after a little thinking time I ask the group to call out the answer. So, for example, if my number is 17, a three-stage calculation could be '$24 - 2^3 + 1$'. Alternatively, students could be asked to make up a linear or a quadratic equation so their number is a solution to the given equation. For example, if the number is 9, the following clue could be given: 'My number is the positive solution to $x^2 - 51 = 30$'. An important part of this process is encouraging students to make up questions and decide for themselves the level of complexity of the calculation. Issues of differentiation abound here. If I decide to put the focus on students setting up equations, the outcome could be to recognize that a number is the solution to an infinite number of equations. The 'calculate my number' task is one I frequently use as a precursor to the next, far more active, set of tasks involving students swapping places.

Swapping places

This is probably the task that I have had more fun and laughter from than any other, whether working with 7-year-olds or adults. With students keeping the same number as for the previous task and all the chairs still set out in a ring, I call out instructions such as:

- 'All those who are multiples of three – swap places.'
- 'All those who are one less than a multiple of two – swap places.'
- 'All those who have a number greater than five and less than 12 – swap places.'
- 'All those who are a divisor of 36 – swap places.'
- 'All those who are a prime number – swap places.'
- 'All those who are a square number – swap places.'
- 'All those who are a Fibonacci number – swap places.'
- 'All those who are two less than a multiple of five – swap places.'

There are, of course, many other instructions that will cause students to swap places, based upon triangular numbers, powers of two, cube numbers, numbers one less than a square number, and so on. Asking them to swap places with the person whose number they sum to 30 could be a further rule. If it seems useful to provide students with visual aids, placing sequences of numbers on large strips of sugar paper around the walls will be a useful resource to help students remember and familiarize themselves with the sequences.

At some point I remove my chair and move into another person's place. This means that someone else will not have a chair to sit on. Something that has always occurred, on the dozens of occasions I have used this idea in a wide variety of contexts, is a dawning realization that somebody doesn't have a chair to sit on. Momentarily, the focus of attention is on this person to stand in the space and call out a sequence, thus causing further movement to occur. At this point the game takes on a much greater urgency! Before long people are dashing across the ring, determined not to be the person without a chair. Despite the numerous occasions I have played this game, and the way some students, including adults, have hurled themselves across the ring, nobody has ever managed to injure themselves. However, I recognize that there exists degrees of risk and, therefore, I always check there are no sharp edges or desk corners outside the ring or bags or coats inside the ring that could cause a possible injury. One occasion demanded some creativity in order to include one student who (already) had a broken leg.

What happens after all this activity obviously needs to be considered. How this activity results in students' working on some mathematics is important – although providing students with the experience to see that mathematics really can be 'fun' has its own value. Some continuation tasks are for students to:

- write down as many of the different sequences as they can remember, perhaps discussing them in pairs or in a small group first of all;
- write out some of the sequences and extend them, or perhaps try to take some sequences backwards;
- make connections between multiples and displacements. For example, the numbers 2, 5, 8, 11, 14 are each a displacement of 1 from multiples of 3, or $3n - 1$ (for $n = 1, 2, 3, \ldots$).

A more complex task is one that engages students with the Chinese Remainder problem, an idea I call the 'intersecting sequences' problem.

Intersecting sequences problem

Again using numbers in a ring, I ask students to move according to the rule: 'Find the person, and stay with the person, who is two more than your number.' Obviously the highest odd and the highest even numbered people will not have anyone to find, but these two people will be found by two members of the class. The effect will be to separate the class into two groups: the even $(2n)$ numbers and the odd $(2n - 1)$ numbers (again for $n = 1, 2, 3 \ldots$). Asking the two people with the highest numbers to stay seated, either next to each other, or opposite each other, can be a useful strategy: two resulting groups, the odds and the evens, will then be able to sit down in sequential order, having established what each group of people is 'called' by using the vocabulary of $2n$ and $2n - 1$. A useful way of illustrating $2n - 1$ is to match each person in this sequence with a person in the $2n$ sequence to show that every person in the $2n - 1$ group is indeed one less than a corresponding person in the $2n$ group. Each person is asked to write one of these sequence 'labels' on the back of his or her numbered card.

The next task is similar: 'Find the person who is three more than your number.' This produces the sequences $3n$, $3n - 1$ and $3n - 2$. Again, I work on students' understanding of the idea of sequences, and once the three groups have formed I ask students to call out their numbers in order. Sometimes, for a bit more fun, I ask them to call out their numbers as quickly as possible, or as noisily as possible, or in a voice which indicates their love and passion for their number. This may appear just a bit of 'daftness' on my part; it is certainly part of my classroom management repertoire.

Mathematically, the important concept is for students to see how the sequences 2, 5, 8, 11, 14 ... and 1, 4, 7, 10, 13 ... are related to multiples of three. Under this task they are either in the $3n$, the $3n - 1$ or the $3n - 2$ sequence. Again, students write one of these sequence labels on the back of their card so, at this point, everyone has two labels written down.

Now comes the crunch problem, and this is set up by asking students to form groups by joining with all those people who have *both* the same labels written on the back of their cards. Thus, students with both $2n$ and $3n$ will form the sequence 6, 12, 18, 24 ... or $6n$. Those with both $2n$ and $3n - 1$ form the sequence 2, 8, 14, 20, 26 ... or $6n - 4$. At this point different challenges can ensue, such as trying to find labels for other pairs of intersecting sequences. For example, what numbers are in both $3n - 2$ and $4n - 1$ sequences? The ultimate problem is to try to find a way of predicting what the intersecting label is for any pair of sequences. This will challenge most students – and some inspectors.

Every other person sit down problem

This task begins with everybody standing up and in order from 1 to n. Number 1 sits down, then 3, then 5 and every other person until we get back to the beginning. This means that the first time round the people with numbers 1, 3, 5, 7 ... will sit down, leaving the even numbers standing. On the second time round, and depending upon how many people there were in the original circle, the next sequence of people to sit down will be those either holding 2, 6, 10, 14 ... or 4, 8, 12, 16 ... Using this routine the problem continues until there is just one person left standing. Changing the number of people in the ring is the precursor to setting up the bigger problem, which is to work out what number will be left standing depending upon how many people there are in the ring to begin with. Thus, if there are 27 people in the ring, Number 22 will be left standing. If there are 19 people in the ring, Number 6 will be left standing. Because the outcome of this problem is based upon the powers of 2, there are opportunities here for students to meet these numbers in another context.

There was one amusing occasion when I used this task at a Mathematics for Parents evening (see Chapter 14). Having carried out the procedure a couple of times I suggested, quite randomly, they try to fathom out what number would be left standing if there were 53 people in the ring. At the time I had not worked out the answer, so it was with much amusement when the answer produced was 'Life, the universe and everything' (Douglas Adams, *The Hitchhiker's Guide to the Galaxy*). This problem generates an interesting result and offers mathematical challenges to anyone who finds himself, for whatever reason, standing in a ring of people who each have a number and sit down at various times! Of course, once this problem has been sorted out you might want to see what happen if every third person sits down ...

Other classroom tasks

Frogs and Fleas

There are many other tasks involving students being a number or a 'piece' in a puzzle. The well-known Frogs problem would fit into the latter category, and probably needs no explanation: however, just in case .... The frogs problem involves, say, four people with red hats and four people with green hats all sitting in a row.

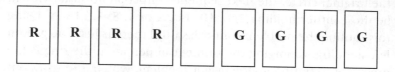

There is an empty chair in the middle and the problem is to work out how they can all swap places using the following rules:

1. Either colour can slide to the adjacent, spare chair.
2. Either colour can hop over one other different colour to gain the spare chair.

This is a cracking good problem; there is also a computer version that can remove the possibility of a more socially interactive experience for students, losing those lovely elements of working together while wearing silly hats. A development of working with the Frogs problem is to see how the sequence of moves appears when there are, say, 15 students on each side of the middle, empty chair. The solution to this problem could be practised as a performance, possibly for a school assembly. To facilitate this, students could be requested to turn up to school wearing one of two agreed colours, wearing green or yellow hats, or sporting red or blue noses.

Another, perhaps slightly less known, problem is called Fleas. The idea is for a number of students in a line to change their position from sitting down to standing up according to the following rules and conditions:

1. Only one flea can make a move at one time.
2. A move is defined as a flea either standing up or sitting down.
3. In order for a flea to make a move the flea to their left must be sitting down and everyone else (or anyone else) further to *their* left must be standing up.

4. The flea on the far left (from the viewpoint of the other fleas) can move at any time. Thus the position of anyone to the right of a flea that is about to make a move is irrelevant.

Thus with five fleas A, B, C, D and E all sitting down, the first move could either be flea D or E to stand up. The problem is how to get everyone standing up using the minimum number of moves. Generalizing the minimum amount of moves for any number of people presents a worthy challenge.

Shifting places on a square grid

This idea is based upon eight students sitting on one each of nine chairs arranged in a three by three square, with the top righthand chair empty. The challenge is for the student sitting in the bottom lefthand chair to gain the top righthand position, and is achieved by students moving horizontally or vertically to the empty adjacent chair. A record can be made of the moves made and what moves different students (counters) make.

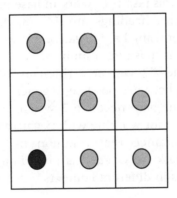

This problem can be extended to any sized square grid, and even to rectangular grids. Again, this will provide extension work for some students.

The next idea is another problem based upon the binary number system, and might be used once students have already become acquainted with binary headings 16, 8, 4, 2, 1.

From binary to denary

This is another standing up/sitting down type problem and is based upon five students sitting in a line, each having one of the values 16, 8, 4, 2 and 1 (i.e. the base 2 column headings). These can be written on big pieces of card, or on hats for students' heads. The task is to make all the base 10 values starting from 1, 2, 3 . . . up to 31, with the appropriate students standing up when their number is required to contribute to each value. This can be a lot of fun particularly if, after any mistake occurs, students are asked to start again at number 1. The feeling of relief and the pleasure generated as the students successfully complete this task is always noteworthy.

An important outcome of such repetition is helping to reveal the structure of the binary system. So the person holding number 1 stands up and sits down as alternate (odd and even) numbers are called, akin to a jack-in-the-box. The person holding number 2 stays standing for two consecutive numbers and sits for the next two numbers, and so on.

An extension to this task is to work in base negative 2, where the first five column headings are 16, ⁻8, 4, ⁻2 and 1. An important reason for using base negative 2 is so we can generate negative as well as positive numbers. In base negative 2, therefore, the value ⁻7 will be written as 1001. With these column headings it becomes possible to generate all values from ⁻10 to 21. Using the base negative 2 system provides students with another context for working with negative numbers. While we can never guarantee that common understandings will emerge from any task we offer, it is important for students to experience concepts in different contexts.

Cuisenaire arithmetic

This idea is based upon Cuisenaire Rods. These are coloured rods with a cross section of 1cm square and of different lengths: the white rod is 1 cm long, red 2 cm, green 3 cm, pink 4 cm, yellow 5 cm, turquoise 6 cm, black 7 cm, and orange is 10 cm.

Again, everybody sits in a ring of chairs and has a number

from 1 upwards. Cuisenaire rods are distributed, in the following way: Number 1 given a white rod (*w*), Number 2 a red rod (*r*), Number 3 a green (*g*), Number 4 a pink (*p*) and Number 5 a yellow (*y*). This colour sequence is repeated, so Number 6 is given a white, Number 7 a red and so on. While the rods are being given out I explain this particular 'world' of mathematics has only five colours and these are given out in the order *w*, *r*, *g*, *p* and *y*. I might ask students to tell me what colour they think they should be given. Very soon everyone has a coloured rod and a number.

There are several possible developments from here: one is to consider the set numbers given to students who hold the same coloured rods. So, for example, after asking all those students holding a green rod to stand up, questions can be asked such as:

- 'What numbers between 50 and 60 would be green?'
- 'What number just under a 1000 would be green?'
- 'What do you notice about the green numbers?'

Such questions are likely to establish the pattern of the unit digits being either a 3 or an 8.

As with the earlier Numbers in a ring task, there is another opportunity to work on number patterns and to consider a linear sequence as a constant displacement from a specific multiplication table. Using the colours *w*, *r*, *g*, *p* and *y*, each person holding a yellow rod will be a multiple of five. So, by asking all those with a yellow rod to stand, and hold up their numbers, students will reveal numbers in the sequence $5n$. I usually write a vertical list on the board and ask all those holding, say, a green rod to stand and call out their numbers in order. This will mean the numbers 3, 8, 13, 18, 23 ... will be listed. Again, concepts of generalizing linear sequences can be worked on as the following patterns emerge:

w	r	g	p	y
1	2	3	4	5
6	7	8	9	10
11	12	13	14	15
16	17	18	19	20
21	22	23	24	25
26	27	...	...	...
$5n - 4$	$5n - 3$	$5n - 2$	$5n - 1$	$5n$

The next task involves simple addition, and I ask two students to stand up, one with a green and the other a white rod. I ask them to hold up their number cards, add them together and see what colour the answer is. Whichever green and white are used, the answer will always be pink, for example, 6 + 3, 1 + 13, 21 + 8 all produce an answer in the pink column. This is because we are operating in Modulo 5, and here the equation $w + g = p$ can be written. Now other equations can be formed, using addition only at this stage. One challenge is to ask students to find all possible equations when two elements are added together.

This idea can be developed to look at the addition of other pairs of colours, and students can be asked to produce a two-way 'Cayley' table:

+	**w**	**r**	**g**	**p**	**y**
w	r	g	p	y	w
r	g	p	y	w	r
g	p	y	w	r	g
p	y	w	r	g	p
y	w	r	g	p	y

A further development can be to look at what happens under multiplication, and again students can produce a 'Cayley' table:

×	**w**	**r**	**g**	**p**	**y**
w	w	r	g	p	y
r	r	p	w	g	y
g	g	w	p	r	y
p	p	g	r	w	y
y	y	y	y	y	y

We are now approaching Group Theory, which is usually the province of undergraduates. However, much younger students will be capable of exploring such structures and can, therefore, access the foundations for working on more complex areas of mathematics.

Another development of this idea is for students to make up

and solve each other's equations. For example: $p + 3r = ?$; $4(2g + w) = ?$; $g^2 + p = ?$, and so on

A further stage could be for students to consider what happens if we only have four colours instead of five: w, r, g and p. In this system the following number patterns emerge:

$w \rightarrow$ 1, 5, 9, 13 . . .
$r \rightarrow$ 2, 6, 10, 14 . . .
$g \rightarrow$ 3, 7, 11, 15 . . .
$p \rightarrow$ 4, 8, 12, 16 . . .

What happens to the addition and multiplication tables now under Modulo 4? Addition tables take on a predictable format: however, this is not the case for multiplication. If multiplication under Modulo 6, 7, 8, 9, 10 and so on is worked on, there is a splendid opportunity for students to produce a display out of their completed Cayley tables. Furthermore, if colours are used instead of symbols, this not only makes an attractive display but the position of the colours also reveals underlying structures in a highly visual way. Students can look for general rules about the structures that exist within the tables, and in particular seek out similarities and differences.

All the ideas suggested so far can easily be used as starting points for further study, and involve students working on tasks over several lessons. The following tasks are much shorter and could be carried out in a few minutes at any point in a lesson.

Subtracting a negative

Subtracting a negative value from something is certainly a highly abstract concept, and I do not believe there is any one 'best' way of helping students to make sense of it. What I offer here are two approaches that might help.

Ask students to line up in order of size from smallest to tallest, and give each person a card on which they write their measured height. The median height can now easily be shown as the person in the middle (or if there is an even number, the value between the two people in the middle). Whatever this is, the idea is to give this measurement a value of zero, i.e. there is no difference between this measure and the median average. Each student is asked to calculate their difference from the median (zero) and write this number as either a negative or a positive value on the reverse side of their card. At this point, everyone has their height written on one side and their difference from the median written on the other.

For the purpose of exemplification I shall assume that the median height for a class containing Jill and Jack is 155cm. If Jill happens to be 161cm and Jack 147cm, a questions such as, 'What is the difference in height between Jill and Jack?' can be posed. The difference between 161 and 147 is clearly 14cm. When these cards are turned over, Jill will have the value $^+6$ on the reverse and Jack will have $^-8$. By using these numbers and turning the earlier question into a computation, we have $^+6 - {}^-8$, and this must also be equal to $^+14$. Students can pose further similar questions and there exists the possibility of holding a discussion about just what is happening and why.

Another way of trying to demonstrate what happens when a negative value is subtracted from something is to set up a scenario based upon the fact that adding $^+1$ and $^-1$ together makes zero. Suppose I want to calculate $^+3 - {}^-2$: I can give each of three students the value of $^+1$ and give two other pairs of students a $^+1$ and a $^-1$. Each of these pairs when added together equal zero, so by adding pairs of $^+1$ and $^-1$ I might be able to convince students we have not added any numerical value to the original value of $^+3$. All seven students now line up holding the following values: $^+1, {}^+1, {}^+1, {}^+1, {}^+1, {}^-1$ and $^-1$. If we now *take away* the two students holding a $^-1$ we are left with $^+5$.

Again, just how deeply students are able to understand this concept and how much their understanding is enhanced by any method or any number of different strategies is a question worth considering. The best we can do as teachers is to try to provide students with a range of possibilities, and to explore why things work as they do. Such an approach is clearly very different to one based upon giving students rules such as 'Two negatives make a positive' – unless, of course, you happen to be adding these two negative values together! This is a further good example of asking students to write about what they have been doing and what they have understood; what started out as a brief period of active people-math can be followed by a quiet period of writing-up time.

Partitions

Ask, say, seven students to form themselves into two groups. They now move according to the rule that at each 'move' one person from each group has to leave their group and join together to form another group. When a 'group' or 'groups' are reduced to only one person they join together with the new group at the next move.

So, if the starting partition is 4 and 3, one person leaves the group of 4 (leaving a group of 3) and one person leaves the group of 3 (leaving a group of 2), and these two people join to form a new group of 2. Thus, the 4, 3 partition becomes a 3, 2, 2 partition. This process now continues as follows:

4	3						First partition
3	2	2					Second partition
2	1	1	3				Third partition
1	0	0	2	4			Fourth partition
0	0	0	1	3	3		Fifth partition
0	0	0	0	2	2	3	Sixth partition

Here the Sixth partition is the same as the Second partition (ignoring the zeros and the order), and therefore a cycle has been formed which will continue to repeat.

Suppose however we start with an initial partition of 5 and 2. What does the cycle of partitions look like now? Different starting partitions and the number of partitions in each cycle can now be explored. Starting with any partition of any triangular number reveals a surprising although understandable result.

Turning inside out

This is another bit of fun, and involves only a small number of students in the first instance (say four or five) holding hands in a ring and facing inwards. The idea is to move without letting go of hands in such a way that they all end up facing outwards, but without hands being crossed over. I have used this at the beginning of a lesson while waiting for a class to arrive, in the middle of a lesson in order to inject a little energy, and at the end of a lesson, posing the problem of generalizing the movement for *n* people, for homework. Asking students to produce a mathematical description is an interesting and challenging task and can lead to a generalization for any number of people.

Place value

I often wonder if the phrase 'place value' might usefully be replaced by the phrase 'the value of the place'. This may sound a semantic whim: however, language is clearly important in making sense of anything. In order to help students make sense of what place value means, I feel that to discuss what value any number takes when it is written in different places in our number system is a worthwhile discussion to have.

This task is not intended to be a lengthy one, and involves students lining themselves underneath place value headings written on the board, for example, *Th H T U • t h th*. If zeros are then written in each of the positions, this helps to show that the zeros are there all the time and we only need to record them when necessary. The idea is to allocate students one digit each, written on a piece of card, and for them to stand underneath one of the place value headings. Discussion can ensue about what number is being represented as digits stand under different column headings. This is clearly where the zeros become important and are necessary to make the digit 3 become 300, 4 become 40 or 5 become 0.5.

The next task involves students moving across columns and again, for a bit of fun, assuming there is one student whose name begins either with a D or a P, one may suggest 'Debbie the dot' or

'Pete the point' joins in. Debbie or Pete can be described as being nailed to the board and being the only person who cannot move when rules such as 'Multiply your number by 100' or 'Divide your number by 10' are called out. Such a task can help challenge the misconceived notion of 'adding' or 'taking away' noughts when multiplying or dividing by powers of 10.

Going out and about

There is always some measure of risk involved in setting up tasks where students have an opportunity to work outside the mathematics classroom, particularly if this involves students being less than fully supervised for periods of time. On a more positive level, I prefer to see such events as opportunities to cede responsibility to students and show trust in them. If I want students to learn how to be responsible, it is necessary to create situations where they are able to act responsibly. The following tasks are, therefore, examples of students working outside the classroom and are based upon creating loci.

Loci

These ideas require a deal of space, and saving them for a sunny day and working outside the classroom adds to the interest. The main idea is for students to become locus points and position themselves according to certain rules. Having an old climbing rope or some bailer twine, a tape measure, some short stakes and a hammer are useful resources. Some rules you might give include:

1. Everyone stand a fixed distance away from a stake in the ground.
2. Everyone stand an equal distance from two stakes in the ground.
3. Everyone stand a fixed distance away from a straight line (this is where the rope comes in handy).
4. Everyone stand on places which are equidistant between

two lines meeting at an angle (again the rope can be used to make the angle, together with a stake knocked into the ground).

5. Everyone stand an equal distance away from a straight line and a point (stake in the ground).

6. Everyone stand so that the sum of the distances away from two stakes in the ground is a constant. (This constant distance can be determined by joining together the two ends of a length of rope that also goes around both stakes).

Loci produced by these situations are a circle, the perpendicular bisector, two parallel lines, the angle bisector, a parabola and an ellipse. Back in the classroom, students can construct these situations using a pencil, a pair of compasses and a straight edge. Understanding the loci created and learning their names is fundamental to this work.

This can be the precursor for further work on loci, and a series of tasks is to consider what loci are created when the conditions of points, lines and circles are used in pairs. Choose pairs of 'conditions', either two points, two lines, two circles, one point and one line, one point and one circle or one line and one circle. The problem is to find all the possible 'condition' diagrams that can be made from all possible pairings. For example, with one point and one circle the following four condition diagrams can be made:

-   point outside the circle;
-   point on the circumference of the circle;
-   point inside the circle;
-   point at the centre of the circle.

Of these four pairs of conditions, two of them are special cases (i.e. the point on circumference and point in the centre). The task now is to draw the loci of all the points that are equidistant between the *point* and the *circle* for each condition diagram. For example, the loci of the equidistant points for the condition diagram, 'point inside the circle' (but not at the centre), is an ellipse.

Given the wide number of different condition diagrams, students can produce several and there exists the possibility for much display work. As well as using drawing implements to produce constructions, there are also opportunities for students to use a dynamic geometry package as a way of enhancing their experience of loci.

Scale drawing

This task is based upon students pacing out certain parts of the school, making sketch diagrams and turning these diagrams into a scale drawing. A starting point is for students to calculate the length of one normal size pace. This might be done by seeing how many paces a student takes to walk a distance of, say, 20 metres. Students could work in pairs, with one doing the pacing out and the other recording the results on the sketch. Pairs of students can be allocated to pace out different parts of the school and create a scale drawing from their calculations when they return to the classroom. A development of this task is for students to use Logo to create a scale diagram.

Another scale drawing task which will cause students to engage with other concepts, particularly rotational symmetry and angle, is that of making sketches of car wheel trims – those things that fly off and can be found scattered on roadsides and hanging off hedgerows. Collecting a few of these as resources for the classroom can be useful. An alternative is for students to make a sketch of one or two of the more interesting designs, take approximate measurements and with this information go back to the classroom and produce a half- or quarter-size scale drawing. Because of the rotational symmetry on many wheel trims, this task requires students to use protractors to replicate them.

Of course, there will be some colleagues who rightly will not want anyone to go near their cars, and gaining permission to take one's class out into the car park to carry out such a task would be both politic and polite. Adorning a classroom wall with a number of spray-painted scale models of different car wheel trims can create a most interesting display.

Teaching and the art of risk-taking

Teaching is a risky business, and as such it is important to know why we may wish to use any idea that involves students not sitting behind their desks. As I mentioned at the beginning of this chapter, using people-math approaches is one way of providing students with variety in their mathematics lessons and this can only be a good thing, especially if such variety is planned and carefully considered within schemes of work. Of course, taking risks can lead us into relatively unknown zones, and we cannot always envisage some of the pitfalls. Nor can we predict some of the benefits and the positive outcomes that occur when we enable students to see that mathematics is not something that only happens while sitting behind a desk. Sometimes we only make sense of something by trying it out: the 'suck it and see' approach to learning and teaching.

Making inroads into a range of teaching strategies is an important part of professional development. When I take a risk, I have to acknowledge that sometimes things won't happen as I had envisaged. However, I have got to try things out if I am going to be able to evaluate the usefulness of any strategy and be able to use an adapted version of an idea in future. If I want students to see their mathematics classroom as a place where different things happen, where variety is a touchstone, and where fun and laughter form an important part of the culture of the classroom, I must be prepared to take some risks. I want my students to understand that from time to time our mathematics classroom is a place where relatively zany experiences occur, and that through such occurrences they engage with mathematics that is interesting, challenging and, above all, accessible.

Using such people-math tasks requires the teacher to take all kinds of risks, and the more positive experiences we have as outcomes of the risks we take, the more varied our teaching styles and the more interesting places our classrooms become.

5

USING
PRACTICAL
EQUIPMENT IN
MATHEMATICS
CLASSROOMS

‘Mathematics is often regarded as the bread and butter of science. If the butter is omitted, the result is indigestion, loss of appetite, or both. The purpose of this book is to suggest some ways of buttering the bread. The human mind can seldom accept completely abstract ideas; they must be derived from, or illustrated by, concrete examples.’

H. Cundy and A. P. Rollett (1952)

The quote above is something I wish I had written! I use it here because it describes a key reason for using equipment to support the learning of mathematics.

What is it about some mathematics classrooms where the use of practical equipment is frowned upon or seen as a distraction to students' learning? Perhaps part of the answer lies in the fact that mathematics is by and large learnt with children sitting behind a desk, and the teacher at the front coaxing out information, giving examples of how to do specific calculations, then providing questions on a worksheet or an exercise from a textbook. Furthermore, given that students are not usually allowed to take manipulatives, such as paper for paper-folding purposes, linking cubes, pinboards or pegboards, with them into the examination room, there may seem little point in letting them use such equipment in preparation to take an examination. Whatever the reason, it seems that using practical equipment in a mathematics classroom is fraught with dangers, adding a further dimension to an already highly complex set of circumstances, and should be avoided at all cost. However, the same students use practical equipment in other lessons, such as art, where a plethora of materials are used, in science and technology-based subjects, and artefacts in history lessons. I am therefore at a loss to understand why the notion of using equipment in a mathematics lesson is sometimes seen as the devil incarnate, creating the potential for student misbehaviour, anarchy and civil unrest!

Sure, I have had the odd paper aeroplane sail through the air in lessons using paper-folding and have sometimes been shot at with a plastic gun constructed from linking cubes; on one occasion, an elastic band orchestra struck up when students were using geoboards. How I respond, how much of a meal or a big deal I make of such an event is related to whether I see it as a challenge to my authority or whether I see such behaviour as a fairly natural part of life in a classroom. Moreover, because such events also occur with undergraduates and sometimes even with PGCE students, I am not at all surprised to see similar behaviours in young adolescents. This may sound like a good reason for not using practical equipment. However, I would be loathe to prevent students from having opportunities to use manipulatives to make sense of certain mathematical concepts because of a minority of students who wish to test my levels of tolerance.

Play is a necessary process, an important precursor to learning. In all kinds of situations we see just how far something will 'go', what its limits are and how flexible something is. We doodle and daydream, play around with ideas and knock things into shape. If this were not the case, some of the most significant inventions we take for granted could be lying dormant and many of the big ideas that affect our lives may have been left unthought.

The case for using equipment

No equipment is imbued with the power to cause anyone to understand anything. This is equally true of a calculator or a sophisticated piece of computer software. How any equipment is used and the purposes behind its use are clearly important issues to be considered at the planning stage of a lesson. Similarly, some students will just not like being given equipment, and as such offering students a choice of whether or not to use any equipment is important. In terms of engaging with the 'K' in VAK (visual, auditory and kinaesthetic), finding opportunities for students to use manipulatives is potentially valuable. Using manipulatives is also important in providing learners with physical models from which they can begin to make sense of abstract concepts. Those students who benefit from kinaesthetic learning experiences will have opportunities to develop an understanding of concepts in ways that may suit their learning style.

We cannot, however, say which learners are likely to receive the greatest benefit from using practical equipment, nor can we classify people as being strongly visual, auditory or kinaesthetic learners: this would be a false separation. In the main, we learn through a variety of ways, according to context, stimuli and how receptive or responsive we are at any time. By providing students with equipment-based learning opportunities, we are certainly drawing upon two of the five senses: sight and touch.

In this Chapter I look at some potential uses for practical equipment in a mathematics classroom, and at some strategies for implementation. In particular, I consider what mathematical concepts and specific skills I intend students to develop, practise, consolidate and understand. I begin with Tangrams, a set of seven shapes that form a square.

Tangrams

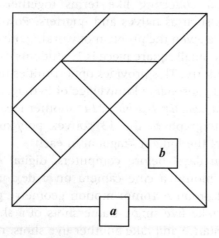

A problem I have frequently used is to give each student the seven pieces mixed up in an envelope and ask them to make a square. This in itself can be a challenge, yet because some will have previously met tangrams they will not be new to everyone; offering further tasks to challenge all students is therefore necessary. Such challenges could be to make other shapes – a parallelogram, a trapezium and a rectangle. While each of these shapes clearly have the same area, they do not necessarily all have the same perimeter (I develop this idea below).

A further challenge is a problem I first came across in *Mathematics Teaching 114*, and is to try to find all 13 possible convex polygons. These are one triangle, six quadrilaterals, two pentagons and four hexagons. As shapes are produced, students could be asked to describe the symmetry properties of each one. Another problem could be to calculate the internal angle sum for each polygon. Again, such a task 'only' requires students to add together angles that are multiples of 45°. This could lead on to working on the connection between the number of sides of a polygon and its internal angle sum.

The next problem is based upon determining the perimeter of each shape. This problem would be more accessible to younger students if they are given the lengths a and b, (as marked in the diagram above), and use these to work out perimeters of the shapes they have made. Such a task provides in-context opportunities for collecting like terms together and adding simple fractions such as halves and quarters. Post-Pythagorean students could be given the problem of working out perimeters if the length of the small square piece is 1. Students can write their answers in surd form. This provides opportunities to practise the use of surds and consolidate knowledge of Pythagoras' theorem. Returning to *Mathematics Teaching 114*, another idea suggested is to draw a scattergraph of the 13 convex polygons perimeter against length of the longest diagonal in each.

In the 'olden days' before computers, digital cameras and Flash, I would mount a cine camera on a dexion frame and students would produce 16mm motion geometry pictures. The process was to take five single frame shots of a shape, move a piece a short distance and take another five shots, repeating this until they had transformed a square, say, into a triangle. The pre-stimulus for this was to show students the *Dance Squared* film. This marvellous short film, produced by the Canadian Film Board, shows how a square can be dissected, transformed, and reconstituted while dancing about the screen, all set to the most compelling piece of music you ever heard ... well, each to our own. Students subsequently produced short films based upon transformations. We had a jolly lot of fun ... then National Curriculum happened!

The value of working with tangrams is therefore in providing the potential for working on a variety of concepts: names and properties of shapes, area, perimeter, angle, algebraic coding, collecting like terms, and calculation with surds, specifically involving $\sqrt{2}$. There are issues here about working in ways that connect mathematical concepts together.

Pegs and pegboards

Playing a game such as Four-in-a-line can provide a stimuli for students to do some work on coordinates and equations of straight lines. One of the positive benefits of students producing lines from the games they play (in pairs) is that students can work out each others' equations. One way of using a pegboard to extend this problem is as follows. Hold up a board containing four pegs in a straight line and physically rotate the board about the centre point through 90°. Defining the point of rotation as the origin, students can be asked to work out how the equation of the line changes. We can ask what happens with rotations of 180° and 270°. We can 'flip' the board over, thereby producing reflections of the line in $y = 0$, $x = 0$, $y = x$ and $y = {}^{-}x$. The challenge is to work out the equations of the new lines formed if we know the equation of the original line. At this point students might be directed to explore combinations of rotations and reflections, and (as in Chapter 4) work on Group Theory is not too far away.

Playing Four-in-a-square might be a starting point for work on vectors, area of squares and Pythagoras' theorem (see Chapter 1). We can also make use of pegs and pegboards for working on problems such as *Frogs* and *Fleas* (see Chapter 4). In this way, students can use the equipment to work on such problems individually, if they find this preferable to wearing a silly hat and working in a group

Pegs and pegboards can also be used for making sequences of shapes in order to explore patterns of growth leading to producing the nth term of sequences. The kind of shapes made using this equipment can be made just as easily with coloured crayons on 1cm-square grid paper. An issue for the teacher to consider is whether offering tactile experiences will enhance students' ability to engage with the underlying mathematics, or whether the equipment might act as a distraction. For this reason I find it useful to give students the choice of whether or not to use equipment; this is also the case when working with pegboards and geoboards. Interestingly enough, I find that given the choice the majority of students do opt to use the equipment.

Using ATM 'beer' MATs

ATM MATs is a resource created by Adrian Pinel and produced by the Association of Teachers of Mathematics. This resource is a set of 2D shapes based mainly upon regular polygons with a fixed edge length. They are made from material similar to that of beer mats and can be used for 2D or 3D work. For making 3D polyhedra, Copydex glue is essential to stick the MATs together to form solids. Not only is this glue quick drying, solids can also be recycled, especially if the glue is applied sparingly in the first instance. For construction purposes, therefore, MATs are easily stuck together using the tiniest smear of Copydex and, because this glue has an ammonia type smell akin to a baby's nappy, it is unlikely that anyone will be encouraged to engage in glue sniffing. I digress.

ATM MATs are definitely for the kinaesthetic-leaning learners and while some written record arising from such work is useful, the most important reason for including this equipment in my classroom is to provide learners with a practical experience to create and explore 3D solids. Providing opportunities to experience mathematics in practical as well as in cerebral ways is important, and MATs offer students a resource to encourage exploration and generally have an enjoyable time. A further outcome of model making is to enhance the classroom environment. Principally, I want students to engage with the resources first-hand and see for themselves something of the intrigue and the beauty of mathematics. 'I came so far for beauty . . .' (Leonard Cohen).

Making 3D models such as the Platonic and Archimedean solids can provide students with much interest. The five Platonic solids (or regular polyhedra) are the tetrahedron, the hexahedron (or the cube), the octahedron, the dodecahedron and the icosahedron. Given that there are two infinite sets and one finite set of Archimedean solids, there will be plenty to go at! Also see *100 Ideas for Teaching Mathematics*, pp. 86–90 (Continuum).

My preferred starting point is to have only equilateral triangle and square MATs in circulation, so the first task is to produce solids made only of triangles, squares or combinations of both. Restricting students to using these shapes generates a lot of solids and these can be explored before other shapes are introduced. An interesting shape to emerge is the cuboctahedron which, as its name suggests, is made from six square and eight equilateral triangle MATs. A continuation task is to consider Euler's rule: the relationship between faces (F), vertices (V) and edges (E) for any polyhedron.

A central aspect of learning mathematics is for students to explore structure, and work based upon polyhedra provides many such opportunities. In the remainder of this section I offer further possibilities.

Euler and truncations

Exploring Euler's relationship is a fairly 'closed' problem; an extension is to explore truncations of solids, which are solids are made by slicing off vertices of polyhedra in two different 'places'. One place is anywhere between each vertex and the mid-point of corresponding edges. The other place is at the mid-point of each edge. So, for each Platonic solid further solids can be made. Looking for connections between F, V and E for each Platonic solid and the truncations opens up opportunities for students to use symbols to describe what happens. The cuboctahedron emerges as an interesting solid created by truncating both the cube and the octahedron at the mid-point of the edges.

Duals of polyhedra

A dual is produced by joining together the centre point of each face of a solid (we can also form duals of tessellations made from 2D polygons). With Platonic solids, the tetrahedron is a self-dual. The dual of the cube is the octahedron and vice versa. The dual of the dodecahedron is the icosahedron and vice versa. The problem becomes more challenging when duals of Archimedian solids are considered.

Finding all the deltahedra

Another interesting problem is to find all the possible deltahedra. These are convex polyhedra made only from equilateral triangle faces, and they form a finite set of solids. Asking students to explore what they are is a significant challenge. This problem can lead to students classifying the solids according to how many faces meet at each vertex. So, for example, three of the possible deltahedra are the tetrahedron, the octahedron and the icosahedron, which have three, four and five faces respectively meeting at each vertex. The other deltahedra are made from combinations of three, four and five faces meeting at vertices.

More problems

Other more complex problems, some of which will challenge older students (including those studying at undergraduate level), are:

- calculating the surface areas and volumes of polyhedra;
- calculating the volumes of the inscribed and circumscribed spheres of polyhedra;
- calculating the dimensions of a cuboid such that when it is sliced through one of its planes of symmetry, the resulting cuboid is similar to the original (the solution to the equivalent problem in 2D is a sheet of A-size paper);
- calculating the dihedral (or the 'solid' angles) of polyhedra.

There are many opportunities here to challenge students to use Pythagoras and trigonometry in 3D in order to make various volume calculations, as well as to calculate solid angles as previously suggested.

The next set of ideas is based upon a piece of equipment I have used in various classrooms and with colleagues who have attended the ATM All-ability Learning and Teaching working group – circular geoboards.

Circular geoboards

Circular geoboards fall into two categories: those with an odd number of pins around the circumference and those with an even number; each has a pin at the centre. Problems are based upon finding shapes that do not have a corner touching the centre pin. Tasks such as finding out how many triangles and how many quadrilaterals there are provide students with a context for naming and classifying shapes they make, as well as creating a systematic method to prove they have found them all. Calculating the angles of the shapes is a further problem. Any angle can be calculated and one way to achieve this is to use the centre pin as a 'construction' point. So with a 9-pin (plus 1 at the centre) geoboard, the smallest angle formed at the centre is 40°. Armed with this knowledge, all other angles can be calculated. The crux issue about calculating angles is to decide if or when to suggest that students use the centre pin to form isosceles triangles; ideally, I want students to think this through for themselves.

The circular geoboard is also an excellent piece of equipment for working on circle theorems, such as:

- opposite angles of cyclic quadrilaterals summing to 180°;
- angles at the circumference subtended from a common chord being equal;
- the angle at the centre being twice the angle at the circumference.

With a 10-pin (plus 1 at the centre) geoboard, diameters can be formed between opposite pairs of pins and this can lead students towards the theorem of angles at the circumference of a circle, subtended from a diameter, being 90°. Regular pentagons can be formed on a 10-pin (plus 1) circular geoboard, and this could be a starting point for work on Golden Ratio.

A real-life circular geoboard

Asking 10 students to sit as equally spaced as possible in a circle and pass round a ball of string usually creates an interesting start to a lesson. The first person wraps one end of the string around a finger and throws the ball to another person a fixed number of spaces away. This person pulls the string tight, wraps it around a finger and passes the ball to another person. So, with 10 people in the circle various outcomes occur, depending upon the add rule used:

Add rule	Outcome
+1	Decagon
+2	Pentagon
+3	10–pointed star
+4	5–pointed star
+5	Straight line
+6	5–pointed star
+7	10–pointed star
+8	Pentagon
+9	Decagon

The symmetry of the situation is likely to emerge and students can be asked to explain why this happens. Further tasks and problems could be as follows:

- Changing the number of people in the starting circle, leading to students generalizing outcomes.
- Seeing what happens when the number of people in the circle share a common factor with the size of the add rule.
- Seeing what happens when there are a prime number of people in the ring.
- Exploring a pair of add rules, say + 2 and + 3 (with 10 people a rectangle is formed).

102

- Calculating the total length of string for each shape made.
- Calculating the angles of shapes formed at the circumference.

I fold up this chapter with some problems based upon paper-folding.

Paper-folding

There are dozens of paper-folding tasks for students to work on a range of concepts. I begin this section with what do with scrap pieces of card and sugar paper that are too big to throw away – you know, those pieces of card where students have automatically cut a shape right out of the middle, leaving the remainder of the card seemingly redundant.

Some centres of a triangle

One way to use the scrap card is to ask students to draw and cut out a range of acute-angled, right-angled and obtuse-angled triangles. We are now in a position to ask students to explore what happens when they fold the sides of triangles in half. This creates perpendicular bisectors where each fold line meets at a single point, the centre of the circumscribed circle. Whether the triangle has three acute angles, an obtuse angle or a right angle will determine if the meeting point is inside, outside or on the edge of the hypotenuse of the triangle. In the latter case students are only a few steps away from seeing the hypotenuse as the diagonal of a circle, so the theorem of a diameter subtending a 90° angle at the circumference is close to hand. We are therefore working on Euclidean geometry, and this kind of paper-folding task is intended to provide access to this branch of mathematics.

Another task is to fold each angle in half to form the angle bisectors: these lines meet at a point, the centre of the inscribed circle. Finding the centroid of a triangle by folding or drawing the mid-point of each edge to the opposite angle is a further task. To begin to make sense of the concept of where this centre point is, students could measure the distances from the mid-point of each side to the centre of mass and from the centre of mass to each angle, and recognize the 1:2 ratio. Indeed, this is a useful starting point for older students prior to developing a vector proof.

A further problem for undergraduates is to explore what happens when the perpendicular bisectors of quadrilaterals are drawn. With asymmetrical quadrilaterals, each pair of bisectors will meet at a point, and these four points will produce the corners of another quadrilateral. Exploring the relationship between the original and the new quadrilateral will be a fine challenge; using interactive geometry software would be useful here.

These paper-folding tasks can also be replicated in a more traditional manner using a pencil, a pair of compasses and a straight edge. All of these mediums and ways of working bring particular aspects of geometry to students' attention. One is not better than another – just different, and as such it is useful for all students to experience all these ways of working: *differences are normal.*

More paper-folding

If I had a penny for every piece of A4 paper I have guillotined down to A5 and A6, into squares and into strips, I would be a very rich person! As it is I have been enriched by the many lessons and sessions I have taught using the spoils of a guillotine.

A range of shapes can be formed from the following starting point. Take an A6 piece of paper and fold it once, so a trapezium with two right angles, a 45° and a 135° angle is formed:

A   B

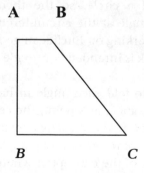

B   *C*

We can ask questions about what properties the shape has. Students can make beautiful tiling pattern displays using brightly coloured paper and sticking the folded shapes onto sugar paper; in this case I would probably cut the paper down to A6 size.

The tiling pattern below is formed by rotation and translation.

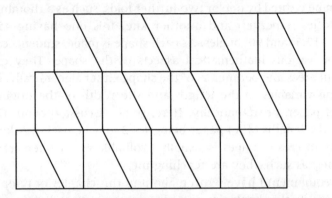

By making the same shape from two different sizes, say A5 and A7, some work on scale factors and centres of enlargement (including negative enlargements) is viable. With three or four different sized trapezia, students can draw in ray lines connecting corresponding points to observe that these ray lines meet at a common point, the centre of enlargement.

By folding down corner **A** a kite is produced; an interesting feature is that it looks much more kite-like once it is turned over onto the unfolded side of the paper.

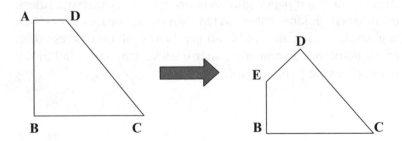

Another feature is that because the lengths of the original trapezium **AB**, **BC**, **CD** and **DA** are 1, $\sqrt{2}$, $\sqrt{2}$ and ($\sqrt{2} - 1$) respectively, the perimeter of the kite is 4. Of further interest is the fact that these calculations can be deduced from the fold lines and do not require any further application of Pythagoras.

However, proving $\sqrt{[(\sqrt{2} - 1)^2 + (\sqrt{2} - 1)^2]}$ is equal to $2 - \sqrt{2}$ is a worthy challenge for some students.

Returning to the trapezium (**ABCD**), there is a range of shapes that can be created by one or two further folds, such as a rhombus, an isosceles trapezium and another kite, this one having 45°, 112.5°, 112.5° and 90° angles. As each shape is made, students can work on various mathematical aspects of the shape. They can work out areas and perimeters of the shape either algebraically, by assigning variables to the length and the width of the original sheet of paper, or numerically. Here, some discussion about the ratio of the lengths of A4 paper being $1{:}\sqrt{2}$ may be useful. Asking students to create shapes is usually profitable and I often learn new ones; as such, they are teaching me.

The equipment I have written about in this chapter or refer to elsewhere in this book requires the department to build up a stock of resources that is affordable and accessible. Stocks of equipment might be stored either in each designated mathematics room or centrally. The latter is clearly the least costly option and requires detailed planning. Having any resource readily available (and this is particularly true for computers and graphical calculators) means being able to make use of them in unanticipated ways. This is important, as we cannot predict when a particular resource may suddenly become useful.

Students need access to lots of resources: different grid papers, string, card, sugar paper, glue, scissors, pairs of compasses, rulers, protractors, linking cubes, ATM MATs, geoboards, pegs and pegboards, Cuisenaire rods, empty boxes of cornflakes, dice, cards, dominoes, clinometres, metre sticks, crayons . . . all in the name of learning mathematics.

6

MENTAL
MATHEMATICS

As a youngster I worked on a milk round. I remember the enjoyment I took from calculating customers' milk bills, frequently amazing them with the speed at which I did this. As an adult I 'confess' I have a habit of filling up the fuel tank on my car, mentally calculating my fuel consumption then setting the trip counter to zero for the next time. Okay, I know I am not alone in doing this! This mental activity is something I do as a simple mind-challenge, and for whatever reason I gain small amounts of pleasure from mentally carrying out such puzzles. However, there are some people for whom 'mental arithmetic' is one of the scariest phrases in the English language.

The increased focus on children carrying out calculations both mentally and with pencil and paper, by contrast to reaching for a calculator, is significant and important. It is significant in terms of raising the debate about the use of calculators in classrooms and perceptions of the impact calculators have upon children's learning. It is important because the outcome of children's achievements with mental mathematics has an influence on both their confidence with mathematics per se and their self-esteem as learners. Confidence breeds competence and self-esteem is crucial in personal development. If children are to perceive mathematics as something they 'can do' and are able to take some pleasure in, then learning to solve problems and puzzles mentally, no matter what magnitude, is an important aspect of raising self-esteem. There are too many adults prepared to voice an inability to do mathematics (unlike having difficulties with reading or writing), sometimes as a measure of kudos. This possibly is a reflection on how some received mathematics and the fear with which some experienced mathematics. The fear some adults have of mathematics and the kind of memories some have about how they were taught it is a problem that must be recognized if subsets of children, of current and future generations, are to experience a lesser fear. Here is an anecdote relating to some work I did with an adult studying on an initial teacher teaching course.

I was working with a student, helping her with 'basic' mathematics. We had met on two or three occasions earlier to go through concepts to help her 'pass' the Teacher Training Agency mathematics test; we were looking at errors she had previously made. The student shared with me her frustration and anger about how hopeless she felt to be at mathematics. In response to her difficulties I focused on how she might try to unravel the meanings behind certain questions and where she might begin to answer them. Many questions required mental multiplication, seven eights, nine threes etc. Each time she resorted to counting on her fingers.

Here then was a student who was totally unconfident about her mathematics and angry as to the reasons why. At one point her anger spilled over into tears: these however turned out to be tears of joy and pride. She told me how another tutor had visited her teaching practice school to collect information from the children about some work they were doing. For some reason the children told the tutor how much they liked their new teacher and how good she was at mathematics, how she never got angry and how she carefully helped them with their mathematics. 'Why', she demanded to know, had she not been helped and encouraged to make sense of mathematics when she was a child at school? 'Why' had she been made to feel 'stupid'?

While mathematics is something that largely takes place in our heads, it does so both academically and emotionally. To separate affective dimensions from cognitive domains is to ignore the fact that what we learn is dependent upon how we feel about what and how we learn. Of course, we write down and write up mathematics: however, in the main, mathematics is a discipline we often see and carry out in our mind's eye.

So, what do mathematics lessons look, feel and sound like?

What expectations or perceptions do students have about mathematics lessons, how they look, feel and sound? In what ways do students come to learn to behave, mathematically? Answers to these questions will be influenced by the expectations individual teachers have and the culture they seek to create within their classrooms. If students expect to carry out calculations mentally in a mathematics lesson, so that over time they come to 'know' about facts and routines, this is a reasonable expectation to have. However, we cannot expect all children to be able to carry out calculations at the same speed while the clock is ticking. Students must be encouraged to 'know' about mathematical calculations in gentle, supportive, non-competitive ways.

A typical example of coming to 'know' about mathematics relies upon students becoming confident, over time, about certain facts. There are many facts that students will benefit from being able to quickly recognize and come to know about, without having to stop to work out.

Take the number 13 for instance:

- 13 is the sum of two squares ($2^2 + 3^2$).
- 13 is a prime number.
- 13 is a number in the Fibonacci sequence.
- 13 is the square root of 169.
- 13 is the number of cards in a suit in a pack of cards.

Of course, the idea could be reversed, i.e. 'If the answer is 13, what could the question be?' Helping students to establish a working knowledge about number facts, so they see the different properties that numbers have in different contexts and different sequences, is a key aspect of building confidence. Doing calculations mentally as well as by writing something down are both important. Mental mathematics, however, is all too strongly associated with numerical calculations. These are often carried out by learners at a speed determined by someone else, either the teacher or, with regard to mental tests, by a government quango via national tests. While being able to carry out such calculations is undeniably important, it is also important to recognize that 'in the real world' if we need to do a calculation we do not have someone standing over us with a stopwatch. In the real world we may make an estimate, we may ask somebody else or we may consult the chart in the DIY store. If we need an accurate answer we may choose to use a calculator. We may decide to carry out the calculation later when we have more time to think about it.

Of course, many children enjoy the challenge of working out answers to mental arithmetic questions at speed. However, danger lies in children comparing themselves with each other and this can be particularly difficult for children who need more time to work something out in order to arrive at the required answers. In such situations the competitive nature of a mental arithmetic 'test' might well offer 'success' to those children who usually answer most questions correctly, but we must also consider the impact on those children who do not answer very many questions correctly. In a more positive way, children can be encouraged to share methods they use, help one another construct mental methods and support each other in the refinement of calculation methods; such approaches are currently used in some schools for the greater benefit of students. There is a range of tasks which can be introduced, such as imagining number lines, number grids and conceptions of infinity. Peter Lacey's article in *Mathematics Teaching* (1998) offers a rich vein of mental arithmetic tasks.

It is indeed a complex situation, and more so if we consider a different aspect of mathematics that we work on in our mind's eye: geometric imagery. Balancing activities between arithmetical and geometrical work will provide students with broader perspectives on mental mathematics. The following ideas, therefore, consider mental mathematics as mind-imagery, taking a geometrical perspective.

Mathematics and imagination

As discussed on p. 44, *Mathematics from 5 to 16* has one of its aims as 'Imagination, initiative and flexibility of mind in mathematics'. The next section develops the power of the imagination, of mathematics in the mind. I begin with a mental activity designed to turn a square into a circle. This idea is something I frequently use with groups, sometimes as a starter task for trigonometry. Having invited the students to close their eyes I ask them to create pictures in their heads: Okay, here goes – close your eyes ... no, don't do that ... you won't be able to read the next bit! Just imagine you have your eyes closed and are responding to the following:

1. Imagine a square.
2. Shrink it, enlarge it, decide upon its colour.
3. Place your imaginary square on your forehead and make sure you can see its four edges.
4. Now draw in the two diagonals of the square.
5. Look at the point where these diagonals meet and place a drawing pin (ouch).
6. Now start turning the square anti-clockwise, very, very slowly about the drawing pin.
7. Now speed up the rotation, go faster and faster.
8. Rotate even faster, as fast, as fast as possible ...
9. Stop, open your eyes.

What did you see? With a bit of imagination it is possible to turn a square into a circle.

I often use this imagining as a starter task for trigonometry, where half the length of the diagonal becomes the rotating arm and can be placed on a coordinate grid. We subsequently draw up cosine and sine tables, or the horizontal and vertical coordinates that describe the position of the end of the rotating arm (see Ollerton and Watson 2001, 113–15).

Some other questions we might ask in order to progress to work on other concepts relating to circumference, area, percentage increase and loci are:

- How is the circle related to the square?
- How does the perimeter of the square compare to the circumference of the circle?
- What is the percentage increase of the perimeter of the square to the circumference of the circle?
- How does the area of the square compare to the area of the circle?
- Suppose the drawing pin is placed in the corner of the original square, what happens now as the square is rotated?
- Suppose the drawing pin is placed halfway along the edge of the square, what happens now?
- Suppose I rotate the square about one of its corners and trace

quite right! I take the poster down and give everyone an hexagon MAT. Using this as an outline (which is the 2D ou of the shape on the poster) I ask them to try to replicate they have discussed and seen. This is frequently met 'anguished' moans: however, having got over the initial sh students beaver away at the task and this offers further pair small group discussion about what the picture looked like. B end of a lesson there are various drawings and students usually keen to have a second look at the poster to check ou accuracy of their drawing.

The ideas I have described in this section might be use stimuli for 'one-off' lessons or as starting points for n extensive pieces of mathematics. The most important issu variety in offering students tasks that require the use of diffe skills and aptitudes and to work in different ways. Underpinn such tasks is the value of imagery, discussion and the powe enjoyment. When learners see mathematics as something to embraced, something they can enjoy, they are less likely to re in fear when they find other aspects of it difficult a challenging. Reducing the fear of mathematics and replacing with fun and enjoyment is a sizable and wholly desira challenge, but not an impossible one.

out two concentric circles formed by an adjacent corner and the opposite corner of the square. What is the circumference and area of each circle?
- Suppose we rotate two concentric squares where one square is half the edge length of the other?

While different students will be able to hold different amounts of information in their heads, there needs to be a point in proceedings where discussion about what different students see turns into a sketch or an accurate drawing. This change of task is valuable in terms of adding variety to students' mathematical experience. The unanswerable question is when the mathematics in students' heads needs to become diagrams on pieces of paper.

Intersecting circles

This involves asking students to imagine two circles of the same size moving towards each other along a line which joins the centres of the circles together:

1. Imagine two circles of the same size on either side of your forehead.
2. At the beginning the circles are not overlapping.
3. Now imagine a line joining the centres of the circles together.
4. Move the circles towards each other so the centres stay on the line just drawn.
5. When the two circles touch each other make them move very slowly.
6. When they just overlap stop and draw dots at the points where the circles intersect.
7. Form a shape by joining lines from the centre of each circle to the intersection points.
8. Start the circles moving again so the centres come closer together.
9. Stop and once again join lines from the centres of the circles to the points of intersection.

One might use the image of an elastic band around the four points, so describing a more dynamic image. Questions can be asked about the shapes formed, how their perimeters compare, how their areas compare and what happens when circles of different sizes move towards each other (thus producing kites instead of rhombuses). Trying to answer questions about perimeter and area again requires students to record what they saw and, in the first instance, to consider particular cases, given the radii of the circles and the distance between the centres.

Slicing a square

This mental imagery task is about creating shapes from two isosceles right-angled triangles (IRATs) formed by slicing a square down one of its diagonals.

1. Imagine a square with opposite pairs of sides sitting horizontally and vertically on your forehead. Slice the square down the diagonal from top lefthand to bottom righthand corner. (At this point students can be asked to say what shapes they have formed in order to establish what properties the shapes have and what sizes the angles are.)

2. You are going to move the triangle on the right hand side of your forehead and keep the other one still; imagine the left side triangle is red and the triangle on the right is blue. Slide the blue triangle down the diagonal until the top left hand corner is just touching the bottom right hand corner of the red triangle. Now slide the blue triangle along the bottom edge of the red triangle until the two edges are joined together.

3. What shape is now formed?

4. Now slide the blue triangle horizontally to the left until the two 90° angles are just touching at a point. Now rotate the blue triangle clockwise about this point through an angle of 90° until the blue triangle touches the red triangle edge to edge.

5. What shape is now formed?

Within this sequence of movements all the shapes that can be formed by joining two IRATs full edge to full edge will have been made. This could be a precursor to a systematic exploration of the shapes formed by joining three or four IRATs.

Moving from mental imagery to recording what happens next could be a paired or small group task. Students might be given the brief of finding out as much information as possible about the shapes that are formed, and preparing a poster to present what they have found.

Hot seating and the Great Dodecahedron

The final task in this section is one that requires a certain resource (published by Tarquin), 'The Great Dodecahedron' poster – a beautiful picture printed in six colours.

The strategy I use is sometimes referred to as 'hot seating'. I arrange the class in a couple of arcs around the board with the poster displayed on the board, and next to it an empty seat. This is the hot seat and students are invited to come and sit in this seat when they have something to say about the poster to the rest of the class. I insist that once in the hot seat students literally have to sit on their hands, so they have to describe what they see without being able to draw hand pictures or point to particular points on the poster.

This task always generates a great deal of fun and laughter as students in the hot seat go through mental contortions to explain to others what they can see. Because of the complexity of the poster and the wide range of both 2D and 3D shapes that can be seen, there are plenty of opportunities, depending upon the size of a class, for all students to offer contributions. Clearly, some prefer not to sit in the hot seat and this is something I must take into account.

Usually after the poster has been discussed for 15 or 20 minutes, or when contributions appear to have dried up, I ask the question: 'So, do you think you know a lot about this picture?' Because students are usually wise to such rhetorical or loaded questions, I usually only get a quizzical response ... they know that something else is about to happen ... and they are

7

Mathematics Across the Curriculum

How many times have we heard a student exclaim something such as, 'Why are we writing in a mathematics lesson – that's what we do in English!'. Behind such a statement lies a worrying feature of our secondary education system, where subject boundaries are largely fixed by timetables and students experience different subjects in different doses with different teachers in different classrooms. It is hardly surprising, therefore, that students section off their learning into discrete packages; the most worrying feature of this is a seeming inability to transfer knowledge learnt in one subject area to another. However, when coursework as a component of assessment at GCSE level first came into being in 1986, many students had to learn to write (as in writing words and sentences) about some of the mathematics they had been exploring. In effect, coursework became a natural context for students to transfer skills from one subject area to another.

This section is about places where mathematics naturally occurs in other contexts. For pragmatic reasons I look in detail at connections between mathematics and art, providing an example of how it is possible to explore places where mathematics exists and how natural links can be made. I then suggest examples where mathematics or mathematical processes naturally occur in other subject areas.

Mathematics and Art

There are a multitude of connections between art and mathematics, many being geometric by nature. There also exist numerical connections, particularly through the Golden Ratio, which itself is strongly connected with geometry. So, for example, in a regular pentagon the ratio of the length of a diagonal to the length of the side is 1.62 (to two decimal places), and this is an approximation to the Golden Ratio.

It is worth stating clearly at this point that just because such connections exist I am not advocating that the art teacher should turn an art lesson into a mathematics lesson, nor that the mathematics teacher should focus in great depth on the artistic. However, if we are aware of such connections, then helping students become similarly aware is one way of providing a coherent, joined-up education. For the art teacher, therefore, to give some mention, where appropriate, to mathematical connections, and for the mathematics teacher to give value to the aesthetic aspects of mathematics, can only enhance students' overall learning experience.

Any work involving tessellation designs can be aligned to art, and the work of the Dutch artist M. C. Escher provides classic examples of this interface. Exploring which shapes form regular and semi-regular tessellations, classifying a tessellation, considering sizes of angles of the shapes involved, and asking questions about whether a tessellation is based upon reflections, rotations, translations, and/or combinations of these may be considered as more mathematical. However, providing students with opportunities to make shapes and 'play' with tessellations is less distinguishable from art, while simultaneously being an important precursor to further mathematical investigation.

Tessellating quadrilaterals using vectors

This idea starts by drawing any quadrilateral with vertices on the intersection points of a square grid. The next step is to describe the shape using vectors by defining each of the four line segments. For example, using the quadrilateral below, we have:

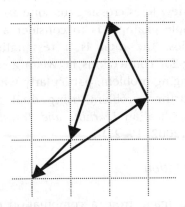

The vectors (moving clockwise around the shape) are:

$$\left\{ \begin{array}{c} \rightarrow \end{array} \binom{3}{2} \leftrightarrow \binom{^-1}{2} \leftrightarrow \binom{^-1}{^-3} \leftrightarrow \binom{^-1}{^-1} \rightarrow \right.$$

The arrows show how adjacent pairs of vectors are connected. The first and the last vectors, as described above, are also adjacent. Checking the sum of these vectors is $\binom{0}{0}$ may be useful.

Once these vectors have been established, the idea is to draw line segments on a grid determined by the vectors. The 'rule' for drawing these is to start with any vector, draw the line and move to either adjacent vector, then draw this line. Continue this process, sometimes going over a line already drawn, and after 20 or so lines have been drawn, the tessellation pattern 'should' become clear! Because any quadrilateral will tessellate, this vector method will also produce a tessellation, made from a combination of translations and rotations of the shape used. Tessellating triangles using this vector method will be a simpler process, but the designs produced are not nearly as interesting as those based upon quadrilaterals.

Having carried out some work with tessellation we might wish to focus attention on angles around a point, or to consider the kinds of transformations involved in making a design. We may want students to explore dual tessellations. This is where the 'centre' (the centroid) points of shapes in a tessellation are joined together with the new lines crossing just one arc of the original tessellation. A simple example is to consider a tessellation of equilateral triangles; the dual is a tessellation of regular hexagons. Looking for connections between a tessellation and its dual is a challenging problem, particularly with semi-regular tessellations. A further problem using dual tessellations is described in my publication *Learning and Teaching Mathematics Without a Textbook* (2002, 19–21).

An Eritrean tessellation

The tile below is a made from a combination of non-regular pentagons and kites and is the basis of a pavement design on

Liberation Avenue in Asmara, Eritrea, a country where I had the enormous privilege to do some work.

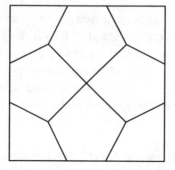

A tessellation of this tile produces the following pattern, and this provided me with the stimuli to explore the geometry of the tile – to my colleagues' amusement (or perhaps bewilderment?).

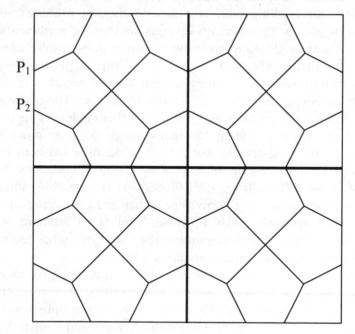

Exploring the geometry of this tile I noticed that by extending the two sides of the pentagon starting from points P_1 and P_2 they go to opposite corners of the square. One angle in each pentagon is 90° and each of the other four angles are equal (112.5°). This makes the obtuse angle of each kite 135°. I also explored the dual of this tessellation.

Whether this design is used as a stimulus for an art, mathematics or even geography lesson is largely irrelevant. What is important is recognizing the cross-curricular possibilities and, therefore, the value of departments communicating with one another about common ideas, and the possibility that connections between disciplines can be made explicit to students.

Mathematics in general across the curriculum

Science and mathematics share many common features. Students carrying out simple experiments or using the kind of information found on the side of a cereal packet provide a useful context for working with real data, crunching numbers and drawing graphs. The issue, however, is not that the mathematics department 'ought' to teach students how to draw graphs before they need such skills in a science lesson; this suggests a linear approach to learning, and suggests that students readily transfer such knowledge from one subject area to another. The best way for students to learn to draw a graph is for them to have a specific need or context for doing so; such contexts occur as much in science and geography lessons as they do in a mathematics lesson. Similarly, when students write chemical equations like $H_2SO_4 + Mg(OH)_2 = MgSO_4 + 2H_2O$, there exists a valuable context for students to develop knowledge of balancing equations. It is important to make such processes explicit so students see connections between the equations they meet in science lessons and those they meet in mathematics lessons.

In both primary and secondary schools, students learn about coordinates. This system is similar to writing six-figure grid references on a map. One difference is that in geography lessons students are likely to be working with real maps and as such they have real information to use, apply and make sense of the coordinate system. The same is true for students collecting and working with data in mathematics lessons that arises more naturally in personal, social, health/citizenship, historical and geographical contexts. Rather than the mathematics teacher using spurious contexts from a textbook, there exists a wealth of real data that students are presented with in other curriculum areas. Such data can be used for students to consider the actual mathematics involved in displaying data, say, in a pie chart. The process, however, is by no means a simple one, and for a history teacher to lose the thread of students' exploring issues from a historical perspective to learn the mechanics of constructing a pie chart is likely be somewhat of a distraction. Problems occur when students do not have the conceptual knowledge required to produce information in a pie chart and this might well cause frustrations, possibly resulting in off-the-cuff comments such as, 'Don't they teach you this in mathematics?'. Of course students are taught how to draw pie charts in mathematics lessons: however, there are reasons why students suddenly cannot draw them in another lesson. These include:

- The class was about to be taught them next week.
- Students cannot remember how to draw one.
- Students struggle to transfer knowledge gained in a mathematics lesson to other subject areas. This may not be surprising, as students often struggle to transfer what has been learnt in one mathematics lesson to another mathematics lesson!
- There exists a mismatch between what has been taught and what has been learnt.

Drawing a pie chart is one of the most common methods for displaying data used in several areas of the curriculum, and I suggest one approach that may help.

Pie charts from bar charts

A context might be Year 7 students in a history lesson studying a typical day in the life of a medieval monk. The teacher may want students to make comparisons between how they and a medieval monk typically spent time on different tasks by displaying comparative information on two pie charts.

123

The model I offer here is simple yet robust, and the example is based upon converting three groups of data **A**, **B** and **C** – from a bar chart to a pie chart (I have chosen just three pieces of data for simplicity; there could be more).

The bar chart reads as follows:

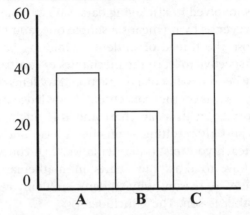

The next step is to join all three bars together into a single, complete strip. Alternatively, **A + B + C** is found and one long strip is cut out and divided into the different sizes.

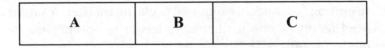

Now join the ends together so the complete strip forms a circle (or a hollow cylinder).

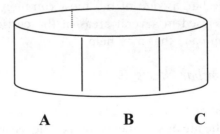

Because the complete strip forms the circumference of the circle, sectors can be drawn from the centre of the circle to each of the join lines between strips **AB**, **BC** and **CA**. These sectors then produce a pie chart representation of the original bar chart.

Although this method circumvents the need for students to carry out the calculation of dividing the combined data total into 360°, it does not lose any integrity in terms of the underlying mathematics. Indeed, such a method could provide a starting point in a mathematics lesson for students to make greater sense of the process involved in drawing a pie chart.

Helping students to see connections between what they do in mathematics lessons and the contexts of other subject areas, to make explicit the implicit, is important if students are to make sense of the world of education. As such, it is valuable for teachers from different disciplines to share the kind of mathematical skills they require students to use; in this way, departments can work together to create a coherent experience for students. This obviously takes time, and devoting 'closure' days for teachers to work together on cross-curricular issues is essential if such sharing is to be feasible.

8

TEACHING
MATHEMATICS
THROUGH 'REAL-
LIFE' CONTEXTS

Mathematics teachers are frequently advised of the importance of using real-life, everyday contexts in their teaching. This advice would seem to make good sense, particularly if students become more interested with and engaged in mathematics as they see relevance in the work they are asked to do. I also strongly argue that recognizing a need and finding ways of meeting that need provides powerful stimuli for action. However, I have concerns about mathematics being learnt only for utilitarian reasons. The quote from Courant and Robbins (1941) given in Chapter 1 continues as follows:

> Without doubt, all mathematical development has its psychological roots in more or less practical requirements. But once started under the pressure of necessary applications, it inevitably gains momentum in itself and transcends the confines of immediate utility.

As with most aspects of learning mathematics, a balance has to be struck between the practical and the aesthetic, the functional and the elegant, the concrete and the abstract.

So, where does mathematics occur in everyday, real life?

When I am cooking, I don't carefully measure out the ingredients: it's more a case of lobbing in a spoonful of this and a pinch of that – sometimes cursing myself for forgetting to add a teaspoon of something else. I learn to cook through a combination of interest and necessity. At most, mathematically speaking, I use rough and ready estimation skills based upon trial and error and, at best, trial and improvement. When I am walking the hills I don't explicitly relate my knowledge of the coordinate system to grid references on the map. This was particularly true when I found myself doing a circular route over Skiddaw recently. The weather conditions gradually deteriorated and before I reached the summit I was in thick cloud. Unwisely I had put the wrong map in my rucksack; I did, however, have a compass and fortunately met another walker at the summit cairn who did have the correct map. At that moment the most important skills I needed to call upon were to work out, and remember, a couple of bearings and estimate a distance to walk before changing direction. Given that angle within trigonometric contexts is measured as an anti-clockwise rotation from the horizontal and as a bearing is measured clockwise from the vertical, one could end up in a state of some confusion. As such my mathematical knowledge may have militated against a safe descent! I don't remember being taught bearings in a practical, useful way ... instead, there were lots of questions to answer from lifeless, soulless textbooks.

The amount of mathematics I learnt at school and use explicitly or overtly in my daily life (outside teaching) I would quantify as infinitesimal. If we stop to ask ourselves what mathematics we need and regularly use in our daily lives, we would struggle to find anything beyond basic computation and estimation. Of course, some people do regularly use complex mathematics in the work they do. Yet for most of us, the highest level of everyday mathematics we use is to add, subtract, multiply, divide, estimate and approximate, and nearly all of these are carried out mentally. Rarely do we use a calculator, as to do so would break the flow of what we are doing and may become a distraction to the task at hand.

Teachers' adult contexts of buying fuel, working out tax returns and calculating VAT are rarely the immediate concern of many adolescents. They have different concerns that exist in the present, or at best in the near future, and are driven by magazines, radio and television; action is often determined by peer group pressure and being 'good' at mathematics may not appear to be particularly 'cool'.

Finally, 'real' real-life contexts do not exist in the pages of a textbook; indeed, long before any textbook appears on shelves, so-called real-life contexts will be out of date and lack reality. Furthermore, when real-life information appears in any published scheme, such data is usually taken out of the real context from whence it came, so only a small part of the context is revealed, creating further decontextualisation.

We can of course ask the same questions of other disciplines: what is the value of studying *Hamlet* or knowing what happens when we mix an acid with an alkali? I could similarly deconstruct and devalue the art education I received: however, because my art teacher made the lessons interesting and enjoyable, challenging and fun, I only have praise and good memories of art. This despite the fact he was an ardent Rovers fan in a Claret and Blue town, an important consideration as a football-mad adolescent (possibly *the* most important).

This leads to two key questions:

1. What do teachers do to make any subject worth studying?
2. What place is there for using real-life information in a mathematics classroom?

What do teachers do to make any subject worth studying?

Seeking to create a classroom culture intended to help some students overcome a tendency to dismiss the value of learning mathematics is a challenge. Much depends upon what kind of places we want our classrooms to be, and how we seek to challenge students' intellects. I place value on the importance of challenge and humour; above all, I want my classroom to be a place where students enjoy being, as I believe they learn mathematics more effectively if they see my classroom as an 'okay' places to be in. Constructing a classroom culture depends upon building trust and mutual respect. As students gain greater trust, they become more prepared to try out all kinds of ways of working. I make no attempt to define or 'dress up' mathematics in pseudo contexts that are in danger of reducing the integrity of mathematical thinking.

As discussed in Chapter 1, posing the question 'What is the point of learning mathematics?' provokes a range of interesting responses; students are perfectly capable of coming up with their own reasons. One outcome of using this or a similar question is that rarely have I been asked it in a threatening or confrontational way by students; we are in the business of teaching and learning mathematics together. Such discussions inevitably enhance the culture of the classroom, creating a sense that 'this' classroom is about challenging the roots of why and what they are learning and setting up and solving problems.

The strength of the web of relationships that exists in every classroom between teachers and students, students and mathematics, and teachers and mathematics is of paramount importance. Using such relationships to build a culture of learning, based upon problem-posing and problem-solving, underpins the rationale why anybody might engage in lessons about trigonometry, *Twelfth Night* or the Russian Revolution.

What place is there for using real-life information in a mathematics classroom?

While problem-solving is the approach I use most commonly for teaching mathematics, this does not preclude the use of real, real-life contexts. Most of these provide access to data-handling concepts, such as the use of newspapers, particularly the sport and weather pages. An important aspect of using the latter as a resource is to take the whole of the weather page into my classroom and not make any attempt to select specific information.

The weather page

Something that became a habit, verging on an obsession, was to collect each day's weather page from a newspaper for weeks, months and eventually years! I would carefully cut out and place the weather page for each day in envelopes, different ones for different months. This meant that I had a resource for students to use to chart changing patterns in weather, tides, temperatures, lighting-up times and so on. For students to see graphs emerge over time, particularly a graph showing changes in high and low tides, requires access to a lot of information. An interesting planning/cross-checking task is to see how much data-handling, as detailed in National Curriculum, can be accessed through the variety of types of information found on the weather page.

One strategy I use at the beginning of the 'Weather' module is for everyone to sit in a ring, each with a different day's weather page. I then hold an open discussion on what the information is about; this develops to students deciding upon tasks and problems they might explore using the data. This starting point can provide sufficient work for a two to three-week period; my role is to help individuals and small groups use data-handling processes and through this to teach a range of different data-handling skills.

Using the weather page provides students with 'real' up-to-date information, and is a marvellous resource in mathematics, geography or science classrooms. The massive amount of information on the weather page is an easily collectable resource and automatically supports cross-curricular ways of working. Below are some tasks students might work on.

1. Drawing a centigrade to fahrenheit conversion graph.
2. Exploring the changing length of daylight (measured from sunrise to sunset) over a period of time.
3. Exploring the changing length of moonlight (measured from sunset to sunrise) over a period of time.
4. Graphing lighting-up times from the most southerly to the most northerly places in the UK (this would involve students consulting a map of the UK).
5. Graphing lighting-up times to see how they alter for one or two places in the UK over a period of time.
6. Graphing high and low tides for places in the Irish, Celtic and North Seas and the English Channel (this would also involve students using a map of the UK).
7. Holding a discussion about isobars, low and high pressure, cold, warm and occluded fronts.
8. Finding the hottest and coldest places in the world and charting these over a period of time (this is likely to involve students consulting a world atlas).
9. Charting the number of sunshine hours from the most southerly to the most northerly places in the UK (again this would involve students consulting a map of the UK).
10. Checking the accuracy of a five-day forecast.

Having started the weather page module off, therefore, there is no need for further whole class teaching for the remainder of the module. Instead I do a lot of thinking on my feet and intervening where appropriate, offering direct help to some students or suggesting a particular course of action to others. While some students draw grouped frequency graphs, others learn how to convert centigrade to fahrenheit and apply this new-found knowledge to their problem. This approach 'works' in part because students expect to develop a task for several lessons, and this is a key component of the classroom culture.

Because the resource is such a useful one in terms of different students tackling different problems, with many choosing to pair off, a variety of tasks can be carried out, each requiring students either to consolidate previous knowledge or to develop new data-handling skills. Classrooms are incredibly busy and complex places and the more I acknowledge the range of differences that exist, the less possible it becomes for me to be indifferent to such realities. Consequently, it is necessary to plan for diversity and devise a range of strategies to work with students' differentiated learning. There are important issues here about planning lessons that can operate in a variety of ways and take account of students' differences (herein lies another issue that I develop in the final chapter).

Although the next sequence of ideas may be considered by some as 'old hat', my experience of using such measures to develop students' data handling skills has always been positive.

Height, shoe size, head circumference and spans

Collecting data about height, shoe size, head circumference, arm span, hand span, and so on can provide students with a wealth of readily available data that is easy to collect, although clearly needs to be dealt with sensitively ... I always avoid the use of weight as a statistic to be gathered.

One strategy is to give each student a pro forma marked out with each of the measures to be taken and ask them to fill in the sheet anonymously. Whether or not students are asked to record their gender is something that is likely to raise different issues for different teachers. I find that having some tape measures pinned vertically in the room and others horizontally, roughly at shoulder height, enables the data-collection process to proceed smoothly. Once all the data has been collected, I collect individual data sheets and before the next lesson transfer all the information onto one sheet of A4 paper. Ideally, I will ask a lunchtime volunteer to do this task. Of course, all the information can easily be inputted into a spreadsheet file, and making this available to students creates further rich possibilities. Each student is given a code, such as a letter of the alphabet or a Roman numeral. Of course, as soon as the sheet/file is distributed most, and probably all, students try to identify which data belongs to them.

The scene is now set for students to work out different averages, and one task is to find which person is closest to the mean and/or the median average across the different data sets; again, they usually wish to be identified. Using the data to calculate standard deviation by using a scientific calculator or a computer will provide older students with further measures which they can use to understand ideas of spread. Asking students to produce scatter graphs drawn from different pairs of data sets creates plenty of opportunities to practise concepts of range and correlation. Lines of best fit can be drawn, and some students can use their knowledge of equations of straight lines to develop the work further.

One of my more memorable experiences occurred with a Year 9 student who asked if it would be sensible to calculate and place the mean average point on a scatter graph. Next she asked whether the line of best fit would automatically pass through this 'average' point. I was further amazed when she asked if it would be a good idea to draw a second pair of 'axes' through this average point, suggesting that all points to the right and above this point would be above average on both counts. The points in each of the other three quadrants could be similarly described. Powerful stuff!

Two further splendid lessons

Recently I saw a marvellous lesson on fractions and percentages taught by Chris Dodd, who as a PGCE trainee brought supermarket advertising leaflets into the classroom and used these as a real-life resource to encourage students to consider what '3 for the price of 2' and '25% extra' meant. The success of this lesson was based upon the quality of the resource, and the fact it was current information. Chris had clearly thought about using real information to develop students' understanding of fractions and percentages, and also wished to develop a classroom culture based upon interest and involvement.

A further excellent lesson I had the privilege to observe was taught by Beverley John, also a PGCE trainee. She gave each student a mini packet of Smarties and used these to do some data gathering, carrying out an analysis of the colour of the contents. The students were able to extract a deal of mathematics and, given Bev allowed them to eat the information at the end, this was certainly a splendid use of a real-life context as well as a marvellous way of enhancing the atmosphere of trust and building relationships with the class.

Both trainees had thought hard about how to utilize real-life resources in order to create conditions for students to engage with mathematics in real and enjoyable ways. Anything that captures students' imaginations will become 'real' and hence real-life to them; this was certainly the case in these lessons. The 'success' of the lessons could be seen from varying perspectives: interested students, imaginative teaching, students engaging with key mathematical concepts and positive behaviour. Abundantly evident was that all these features were connected.

In this section I explore some of the practicalities of and the principles behind how ICT can support and sometimes undermine learning, and consider why anyone might choose to use ICT as a teaching resource. I restrict my definition of ICT to computers and graphic calculators. Because I have only limited experience of working with interactive whiteboards, I have no intention of seeking to offer any expertise here ... I am however an avid user of overhead projectors.

Having used computers in my teaching since the early 1980s, working from Year 7 upwards with SLIMWAM and SMILE programs, spreadsheets, function graph plotters, Logo, Cabri Géomètre and graphic calculators, I continue to be ambivalent about the value of using ICT in the mathematics classroom. This is not to suggest ICT does not have a valuable place in teaching and learning mathematics (and I notice my initial unconscious use of a double negative here): I am circumspect about the intrinsic or unquestionable use of ICT as a resource. I begin therefore with two questions:

1.   How does ICT help students learn mathematics?
2.   How does ICT help teachers teach mathematics?

To try to answer these questions I look at some pros and cons and invite the reader to think about how any of these resonate with their experience of using ICT as a resource.

Before working on these questions, however, I discuss some differences and concerns I have about two main types of software used in mathematics classrooms. One is software which enables students to explore ideas and take control of how to use it; students interact with the computer, using it as a resource to make decisions about how to proceed with a task. Under this classification I place software 'environments' such as dynamic geometry, spreadsheets, Logo, function graph-plotting programs and graphic calculators. I also place all software produced by the ATM and some SMILE programs in the 'enabling exploration' category. Such resources offer students excellent opportunities to develop mathematical thinking and explore ideas in greater depth than they would were such resources not available. The second classification is software that is pre-programmed, where students answer questions either correctly or incorrectly. They are electronic versions of textbooks that contain repetitive exercises designed to keep students occupied by practising narrow skills. At worst, students are behaving similarly to Pavlov's salivating dogs. They get the right answer and are subsequently rewarded. They get the wrong answer, the reward is withdrawn, and they have to start again.

How does ICT help students learn mathematics?

Like any other resource, ICT is only as good as the context within which it is used. This depends upon the problems students are given to solve, the access learners have to ICT and the way any computer program or graphic calculator is used to solve a problem. Just as a geoboard or Cuisenaire rods are not imbued with mystical powers offering the user mathematical enlightenment, neither are ICT resources. How any resource is used influences the learning achieved; what anyone actually means by 'learning' and what is intended to be 'achieved' as a result of any student using a manipulative, a computer or a graphic calculator is worth considering.

From the student perspective there seem to be three central issues to consider:

- Developing knowledge of different types of ICT software.
- Recognizing when it would be valuable to use an ICT resource.
- Having access to ICT at the point of need.

The way students develop knowledge of how to use any ICT resource is a real chicken-and-egg situation. Do we first learn how to use something then transfer this knowledge to solve a problem, or do we learn how to use something when solving a problem? There is a strong case to suggest that need and context provides powerful motivators for learning. Just how much teaching anyone needs to get them started with a piece of software will vary from person to person. As teacher, I must consider how much I need to offer any student to help them take control of the software. I develop this later in the chapter. I often think, however, about what happened when the girl (p. 212) had her first IT lesson in her new secondary school. To recognize the value of using ICT, students must have knowledge of its existence and the confidence to apply it to the problem they are working on.

How does ICT help teachers teach mathematics?

The best we can do as teachers to help raise students' awareness of any ICT resource is:

- provide students with a working knowledge of what is available;
- cede autonomy to the learners so they can take responsibility for deciding when it would be appropriate to use a certain resource;
- create a classroom environment where students are strongly encouraged to make decisions about what resources they might use.

Creating such conditions requires the teacher to recognize when it is useful to intervene, when to be strongly didactic, when to offer hints and advice and when to stand back and strategically decide not to 'interfere'. Seeking to offer students choice in their learning inevitably means finding problems that encourage students to make decisions about how to proceed and about what approaches and what resources they might use in order to work towards a solution.

This does depend upon accessibility of resources, particularly in the case of ICT. Some schools are fortunate enough to have a 'drop-in' centre, or laptops for students to use. For less well-equipped schools, there are clearly significant planning issues with which teachers must engage; having to book a room some weeks in advance does not facilitate spontaneity, nor does it help students work on the immediacy of a creative thought, nor does it support the conditions for trying out a good idea that a colleague has just mentioned during break time. There are good reasons for having just one computer, as a minimum, in each room; however, this may not be supported by a whole-school policy which uses funding to furnish designated rooms with suites of computers.

Some teaching strategies for using ICT

I have made good use of two strategies in particular to introduce either the programmable and graphing functions on a graphic calculator or a new piece of software to a class. The first, and most potent strategy is one I describe as *Mantle of the expert* and is something I have adapted from the teaching of Dorothy Heathcote, a retired lecturer of Drama in Education. The second is making use of 'crib' sheets.

Mantle of the expert

The strategy is to ask for some volunteers, say half a dozen students, to receive some input over a lunch break in order to learn how to use a specific ICT resource. Here I take the volunteers through a step-by-step process, showing them which buttons they need to press to carry out a basic set of operations. This is an example of strongly didactic teaching and, in this instance, is appropriate to my intention of giving clear, unambiguous instructions. On one occasion I showed students how to write a simple program on a graphic calculator to add two numbers together, and on another occasion how to draw a graph. Using computer programs I showed volunteers how to create the bisectors of sides and angles of a triangle using Cabri, on a different occasion creating sequences using a spreadsheet and on another how to write a simple program in Logo. Each time the half dozen or so students became experts. In the following lesson they were 'charged' with the responsibility of teaching one or two other students what they had learnt. The power of this strategy means having at least a dozen students working together and not needing my assistance; I do not have a full class to teach as I have six other 'teachers' in the room.

Making use of 'crib' sheets

A second strategy is to prepare button-by-button information sheets that detail exactly what students need to do, as a minimum, to get the calculator to draw a graph or to use a spreadsheet to create a sequence. I found this an invaluable resource as it meant I did not need to keep taking a whole class though a set of instructions, something that can be difficult when students are facing a computer screen.

Using such crib sheets also meant I could give one to an individual student who may require some additional input, either because I felt they were 'ready' to use a particular resource or because they were new to a class. Such crib sheets are invaluable as an aide-mémoire. I also made use of such crib sheets when working with lunchtime volunteers, so they had something to refer to.

Teaching Years 7, 8 and 9 children how to program a graphic calculator meant the resource was accessible for future use. Learning how to type in two variables to add a pair of numbers together meant they could adapt this program to carry out other more complex calculations, with any number of variables and different operations. So, when we worked on Pythagoras' theorem in Year 10, the calculators would be available for students to write a program to perform the Pythagroras procedure, either to calculate the hypotenuse or another length in a right-angled triangle. A further development was for students to write crib sheets; they thus had a record of the programs they had written, which would also provide evidence of the work done when assessing coursework folders.

Buying whole-class sets of calculators

Purchasing whole-class sets of simple and scientific calculators and one class set of graphic calculators in my last school was feasible because we did not spend money on textbooks. This did not prevent students from having their own calculators, and frequently parents would ask which calculators we recommend they might purchase.

Being in a position where the whole of a class could use the same calculator meant teachers in the department could prioritize energy for planning lessons around the use of a common resource. For example, in the Year 7 scheme of work, we would explore the order of operations (for instance, whether 3 + 4 × 5 was equal to 35 or in this instance 23), how the different memory keys worked and what the $\sqrt{}$ key did. In the Year 9 scheme of work, we explored functions such as $x!$, $1/x$ and how the % key worked. Year 10 students learnt how to operate different functions in the statistical mode, and as part of a module on indices students investigated the x^y key. Using a graphic calculator in Year 11 meant they could explore iterative functions based upon the following procedure, repeating Steps 3 and 4 a lot of times until 'something happens'.

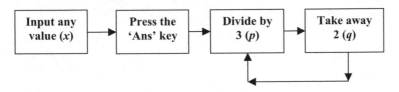

Once the value has settled out (to $x = 3$ in this instance), students can investigate what happens if they begin with a different starting value. Such a key sequence can provide students with a starting point for iteration. At another level, the task could be to sort out what is happening when p and q are changed.

Access, opportunity and responsibility

The confidence with which teachers can plan to use, and the amount of benefit students gain from, any ICT resource is largely dependent upon how accessible resources are and the opportunities for using them. As students become more aware of the types of programs at their disposal, and where the culture of the classroom is supportive of students making decisions about when and how to make use of a calculator or a computer, then ICT is an invaluable resource for learning. The key issue beyond access is for students to understand what they are doing and why they wish to use a certain ICT resource. This is another good example of students learning to take ever more responsibility for their learning. In turn, this requires me as teacher to be clear about why I want this to happen and how I might achieve it.

10

PLANNING A
SCHEME OF
WORK ON
PEDAGOGIC
FOUNDATIONS

In this chapter I consider issues of planning a scheme of work, and five principles upon which a scheme might be constructed:

1. *Creating a modular structure*. I define a module as a collection of ideas and tasks connected by a common theme or broad concept (e.g. volume, area, trigonometry, functions, and so on). For students to access concepts in depth they need time to learn, develop and construct their understanding of concepts and structures; one way to support this is to create modules based upon ideas that 'run' for a minimum of two weeks. 'One-off' lessons might also be interspersed in such a structure to provide variety and give students opportunities to revisit and practise ideas they may have met earlier.

2. *Using problem-solving approaches*. Because mathematics is essentially a collection of ideas used to describe the world and a set of tools for solving problems, students need to experience mathematics in problem-solving ways. Each module, therefore, needs to be based upon exploring ideas and using and applying mathematics.

3. *Access and extension*. This is a recurrent theme in this book. To include all students and create opportunities to learn mathematics, I need to find accessible starting points so everyone can begin to make sense of concepts. Consequently, I need to provide opportunities for students who have different aptitudes and potentials to develop and deepen knowledge and thinking commensurately.

4. *Providing opportunities to practise specific skills*. Within each module students need to have opportunities to practise skills, particularly those emerging naturally in context. In this way, students can see the relevance of practising specific skills by recognizing their emergence within broader concepts. For example, when students use the square root key, say within a module based upon Pythagoras' theorem, there are in-context opportunities to practise the skill of rounding up answers to a given number of decimal places or to a given degree of accuracy.

5. *Pleasure*. One of the strongest emotions that drives us is pleasure (I believe love is *the* strongest and fear follows

closely behind). In order to help students understand mathematics they need to experience the pleasure involved in making sense of concepts: the pleasure of knowing how and why something works. Of course, students will derive pleasure from being in the company of friends and teachers who care and who wish to make classrooms pleasant places to coexist. The challenge for the mathematics teacher is to consider how to make the process of doing and learning mathematics pleasurable.

Constructing a scheme of work: pedagogy and practicalities

To teach in ways that encourage problem-solving, a fascination with mathematics, imagination, initiative and flexibility of mind within the existing climate of narrow testing may require several leaps of faith. Such ways of teaching certainly require mathematics teachers to consider what kinds of approaches, strategies, problems, resources and methods of assessment we want to incorporate into our teaching. For the remainder of this chapter, therefore, I consider how a scheme of work might be constructed to embrace such aims while taking into account external demands.

I offer two examples of modules, each intended to develop a central concept. The first is 'Transformations' and is written with 12 to 13-year-old students in mind. The second is 'Area and Perimeter' and is written for 14 to 15-year-old students. Both examples are built upon the five principles outlined above and a common structure based upon teacher expectations:

1. What knowledge do I expect students to already possess and how might I find this out?
2. What, as a minimum, do I want all students to experience and understand from the module?
3. What extension tasks can I plan to deepen different students' knowledge?

Transformations module

I would expect 12–13-year-old students to have previously worked on reflections and rotations, coordinates, enlargement and possibly translation. I cannot of course expect them all either to have gained the same degree of knowledge and understanding or to have no understanding at all; no-one begins from zero knowledge and everyone has something to contribute, regardless of social and cultural background. Determining what anyone knows is always a tricky business, which is why issues relating to cross-phase liaison and developing strategies to find out what students know, or partially know, are important; I discuss this below. Finding access points to provide opportunities for students to consolidate knowledge, to become confident about new knowledge and challenged to deepen knowledge are essential aspects of the planning process.

I may start the module by asking students to write a few sentences to explain what they already know and understand. I am particularly interested at this point in what key vocabulary students have. Alternatively, I could give them a short diagnostic test. Either of these events could take place at the end of a lesson prior to beginning the module. I could set up a situation at the beginning of the first lesson where I invite individuals to come to the board and write odd words and phrases so we jointly construct a spider diagram as a basis for discussion. A third strategy could be to ask them to work together in pairs to discuss and make some notes on what they understand about a concept. All these strategies are not just intended to help me gain a picture of the knowledge certain individuals already have; it is a scene-setting exercise intended to bring to the surface the central ideas we are about to work on.

Whatever knowledge I ascertain about students' understanding, I am certainly going to pose a problem to cause them to work within the intended domain – in this instance, transformations. One idea is for students to produce reflections and rotations (therefore initially excluding translations and enlargements) of a shape drawn on a square grid by applying rules to transform the coordinate of points that describe the corners of a shape (see

Chapter 12). Further questions could ask students to write about what transformations occur when different rules are applied. Students can be encouraged to make up their rules and in this way there is a strong likelihood that some students will naturally produce enlargements and translations. Within a culture of students being encouraged to ask 'What if?' type questions, such outcomes are quite feasible.

A development is to consider combinations of transformation created by carrying out pairs of rotations and reflections. Some students will be capable of drawing up a two-way table to show what happens when all these different pairs are combined together. At this point, Group Theory is once again not a million miles away – yet I am working with 12–13-year-old students. Suggesting certain individuals explore the structure of such a combination table and consider issues of commutativity of transformations may be appropriate.

I can help students develop ideas about the difference between transformation on a grid (where the grid itself is transformed) and the isometries of shapes, where positions of lines of mirror symmetry and the centre and order of rotational symmetry of shapes are considered. One such problem could be to produce all the pentominoes (shapes made by joining five squares full edge to full edge), something students are likely to have met in their primary school, and find the symmetries for each one. Pentominoes can also be drawn using Logo, and this provides opportunities to use ICT as a tool for solving a problem.

A different task is to consider what shapes are made when a given shape is 'unfolded' along its edges as follows. Consider the asymmetric trapezium in the diagram following. When unfolded it can make four different shapes: two pentagons, a hexagon and an isosceles trapezium.

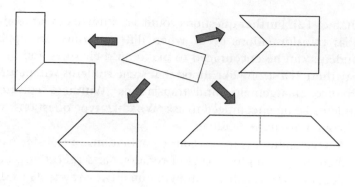

By knowing the angles of the original trapezium, students can work out the angles of the shapes formed by unfolding it. A further challenge would be to find all the different shapes that can be made after unfolding twice. Such a problem can cause students to develop initial ideas of proof in responding to a question such as 'How do you know you have found them all?'.

Within this early planning process of devising a framework of ideas, I need to consider how, where and when ideas might fit into individual lessons, so everyone is exposed to certain ideas. Deciding what, as a minimum, I intend every student to work on is an important aspect of inclusion. Next, I must decide which ideas might be used as extension tasks. For example, I may choose to use the task just described as a starting point for everyone, particularly if I feel this will help students re-engage with concepts previously met. In this way my starter task is intended to form some kind of bridge between experiences they have had and what I want them to go on to develop. Each of the following ideas could similarly be used as tasks for everyone or extension work for some.

1. Asking students to find the planes and axes of symmetry of cuboids or other solids.
2. Returning to a coordinate grid, I can pose problems about ways of changing the ordinates to produce a) translations and b) enlargements of a shape. Such ideas may already have emanated from work students have done earlier.
3. Developing the concept of enlargement, with students considering what happens to the area of a shape when whole number and fractional scale factors are used.

4. Exploring what happens when negative scale factors are applied to a shape.
5. Exploring what happens when a shape undergoes both a translation and an enlargement, such as trying to find where the new centre of enlargement moves to so two transformations can be replaced by a single enlargement. For example, what is the new centre of enlargement after a translation of $\binom{1}{2}$ and an enlargement of $\times$ 2?

I can, therefore, construct a range of ideas and tasks to plan into individual lessons. At this point of the planning process I am more concerned about what a module will look like than having to focus on lesson plans within the module. Turning to the HMI aims in the Introduction, it is important to see how I might meet these in terms of how students experience transformations. I also need to consider how students record what they do, and how I might assess what they have understood.

Area and Perimeter module

The following ideas will already be used in many mathematics classrooms. What might be different is the structure of collecting a range of ideas together to form a module to run for at least three weeks. The starter task could be the context of a farmer's field and the different area of land that can be enclosed from a fixed length of fencing. My preference, however, is to set up the task using a problem-solving approach without any reference to farmers, fields or fences. This is because I question the value of expecting students to reinterpret problems by first of all having to situate themselves within a context that will only be 'real' or meaningful to a small number of them.

The starting point could easily be used with a Year 7 age group, in which case I use the idea based upon finding all possible rectangles with an area of 24cm² and provide students with scissors to cut out the different rectangles drawn on 1-cm squared paper. Students stick their rectangles onto a pair of axes, with the bottom left-hand corner of each rectangle at (0, 0). The top right-hand corner of each rectangle now lies on a smooth curve. I consider below how such a problem might be developed with a Year 10 class, where I expect students to develop the work in greater depth.

Because of the holistic manner in which different ideas are integrated into any module, a range of other skills and concepts will be drawn upon. In the Area and Perimeter module these are:

- working with symbols and constructing formulae;
- drawing graphs (and, therefore, working with the coordinate system);
- squaring and working out square roots;
- rounding-off and writing results to a number of decimal places;
- working on optimization problems, involving maximizing area and minimizing perimeter.

When concepts are integrated into different topic areas and become part of what happens in mathematics classrooms, right from the very first lesson in Year 7, students expect to draw upon different skills and concepts at different times in a range of contexts. This is quite different to teaching concepts in separate, fragmented and isolated ways. Connecting the different skills and concepts together is at the heart of a problem-solving approach, so students are automatically using and applying mathematics.

My starting point for a Year 10 class would be the same as for a Year 7 class – drawing all the different rectangles, with integer values, with a constant area of 24cm². My planning develops as follows:

1. For each rectangle, write the dimensions and calculate the *perimeter*.
2. How many different rectangles (with integer dimensions) can be drawn?
3. How can we be sure we have drawn them all?
4. What are the maximum and minimum *perimeters* of the rectangles so formed?
5. What are the dimensions of the rectangle with the smallest *perimeter*?

6. What *perimeter* values can be gained if non-integer dimensions are used?
7. What does the graph of *length* against *width* look like?
8. What is the equation of this graph?
9. What does the graph of *perimeter* against *length* look like?
10. What is the equation of this graph?
11. What does the *length* against *width* graph look like if a different *area* is chosen?
12. If we know the *area* of the rectangle, how can the minimum *perimeter* be found?
13. If we begin with a constant *perimeter*, what different rectangles can be formed and what *area* does each one have?
14. What does the graph of *length* against *width* look like now?
15. If we know the *perimeter* of the rectangle, what calculation will produce the maximum *area*?
16. How can this kind of calculation be turned into a formula?
17. What does the graph of *area* against *length* look like?
18. Some rectangles have a numerically equal *perimeter* and *area*. For example, a rectangle with dimensions 3cm × 6cm has a *perimeter* of 18cm and an *area* of 18cm^2. What other rectangles have this same property? (This problem is straight from *Points of Departure 3* (ATM, 1989) and is called 'Equable Rectangles'.)

Students could attempt some of these questions with a spreadsheet, and thus ICT skills can be usefully incorporated into the work.

There are plenty of questions here to develop the thinking skills of the highest achieving students, and all the time the only shape under consideration is the rectangle. Of course, it might be appropriate to suggest further problems about exploring areas of shapes other than rectangles, and this will depend upon whether students have any experience of trigonometry, circle formulae and π. If this is not the case, such problems could be revisited when these concepts are being developed.

Ideally, I prefer students to work on extension tasks they create themselves; the richer the mathematical environment, the more likely students are to develop their ideas and ask questions of a situation. Given the inclination children have for asking questions, it is important that in mathematics this is strongly encouraged. Advocating the use of 'What if' and 'What if not' type questions is something that can be incorporated into mathematics lessons as a natural aspect of teaching and learning.

Students communicating what they have done and the teacher trying to find out what students understand

The modes of communication this module can encompass need consideration. There will exist opportunities for whole-class discussion, and throughout the course of the module I expect to have several conversations with each student in the class. Students might choose to communicate outcomes of the work they do through posters, presentations or written work. From the beginning of Year 7, when students write about some of the work they do, they are automatically engaging in literacy skills. A write-up might be done individually, or students could work as a pair to produce a topic booklet.

Deciding upon assessment of students' achievements will also figure under the notion of communication. Much of my assessment will be ongoing and my knowledge of individual achievement will be formed according to the discussions I have with individuals and the work they produce. Students can self and peer-assess, and these are powerful motivators and important aspects of conceptual development (I develop issues of providing formative feedback to students in the penultimate chapter).

Making use of national and home-made tests

A more traditional assessment could take the form of a compilation of questions from past national tests centred on concepts being assessed. A more radical approach is to invite students to write their own test questions and, on the basis of what they produce, construct a test paper to use as an end-of-module or end-of-term assessment tool.

I must, however, be circumspect about what I do with any information, how I 'mark' what students produce and subsequently report back achievement. The following quote from Ken Boston, head of the Qualifications and Curriculum Authority, describes tensions about the outcomes of assessment and the purposes for which it is used:

> A big thing this country has to sort out is the purpose of education. Is it a 'winnowing devise' to sort out the wheat from the chaff, or is it a process that works towards every young person reaching their maximum potential for the good of the nation? There's still a strong current that to have winners you've got to have losers. So for young people to really excel, you've got to have perhaps a majority of young people who fail. That's a confusion that really needs to be sorted out.
>
> *Guardian* (29 April 2003)

Boston raises extremely important issues here and recognizes that we cannot define success within the current system of measures (based upon tests, marks and levels) without at the same time defining failure. However, to redefine success, in terms of real achievement recognized by both teachers and learners, is a worthy and principled challenge. Whether there ought to be greater focus on the psychological wellbeing of the learner than upon 'the good of the nation' is a further issue worthy of consideration.

Problem-solving as the basis for developing modules

Within mathematics any task or problem that begins with or contains questions such as 'Why?', 'How many ...?', 'What if ...?', 'Can you prove ...?', 'What happens when we change ...?', or 'Find some more examples of ...?' are likely to provide students with problem-solving type challenges. The ATM publication *Questions and Prompts for Mathematical Thinking* (Watson and Mason, 1998) is an excellent source for developing questioning strategies. Problems do not always have to represent long and arduous toil, nor do they require students to work individually. The greater the range of problems students meet and work on, the richer their mathematical diet is going to be.

This approach of posing problems based upon accessible starting points, and planning a bank of further questions for those students who are going to need extension work, is one that can be applied to every area of the mathematics curriculum. As I have commented elsewhere in this book, solving problems and puzzles lies at the heart of mathematics, and it is perfectly feasible and highly desirable for all modules to contain a strong element of problem-solving so that students have challenges to rise to and achievements to aim for. Through problem-solving, students automatically use and apply knowledge ... through problem-solving, *everything is connected.*

11

MANAGING A MATHEMATICS CLASSROOM

This chapter is based upon the following two premises:

1. Managing any classroom is a complex business.
2. Physical Education apart, mathematics holds a peculiar place in the curriculum as 'the' subject capable of inducing fear and anxiety in students.

The combination of these premises means that managing a mathematics classroom is sometimes akin to manoeuvring one's way through a psychological minefield. People frequently respond to the word 'mathematics' in particularly negative ways; some appear proud to announce they were never any good at the subject and could never make any sense of the subject at school. One reason perhaps for making such a pronouncement is the confidence that other people will share this viewpoint: it's usually good to have people agreeing with us. In this chapter I look at some of the joys and the challenges, the agonies and the pleasures, of managing a mathematics classroom, with the intention of exploring ways of making teaching and learning mathematics an enjoyable experience. I do not offer any classroom management panaceas, nor do I suggest that there are quick-fix ways of dealing with the complexities of teaching mathematics. This chapter is an exploration rather than an exposition, offering possibilities for consideration rather than prescribing certain methods to use.

Having taught thousands of lessons, I still continue to deliberate on what the constituent parts about teaching are that cause me to leave some lessons feeling splendid and confident that teaching is the best job in the world, while at other times I feel like a raw novice. As such, I do not believe there is a sequence of steps a teacher can follow to become successful. I certainly don't believe in advice such as 'Don't smile 'til Christmas'; such offerings leave this teacher feeling dispirited and I seek to de-bunk statements like this later in the chapter. I cannot accept that teaching can be described by or reduced down to a set of glib statements. If I had the answers I would have taken a sample of my DNA, made an elixir and sold it for many millions.

Something we can do to work on classroom management is to ask ourselves questions about our practice and decide how to answer them. Some questions I have are:

- How do I want students to experience mathematics in my classroom?
- What strategies might I use to support students' learning?
- What resources might I use to aid students' learning?
- What furniture arrangements for different types of lessons might I use?

Other teachers will have their own list of questions. What is important in seeking to become a more effective practitioner is to work through the questions we pose about our practice, and in doing so construct for ourselves an 'inner strength' or a confidence that we take with us into classrooms. This confidence cannot be taught or given, but we can work on it. We can describe the kind of lessons we plan and the ways we respond to students in classrooms (and corridors, and elsewhere) which promote positive working relationships with them. This notion of an inner strength is something we all have, and while there are times we may feel frail and unsure, we know what a 'good' or an effective lesson feels like. It is possible, therefore, to analyse what makes a lesson an enjoyable event. I offer two anecdotes from my practice; the first describes a scenario where I literally had to 'steel' myself prior to a weekly event.

They're coming down the corridor

Last lesson on a Tuesday, one particular year, was often a challenge. I taught a Year 8 group who had a reputation in the school of being a 'challenging' group to teach. For all kinds of reasons the chemistry in the group was problematic and there seemed to be so many ill-at-ease relationships between students. I would often hear them coming down the corridor, arriving in dribs and drabs from a PE lesson. They were still sorting out unresolved issues, arriving over what seemed to be a ten-minute period of time. I had gone through the process of discussing the situation with their PE teachers to try to make their arrival more prompt and less fractious. Despite this, it was always a lesson where I knew I would have to draw heavily on all my experience and at times I still found myself at my wit's end.

The more successful strategies I applied in this situation were quite varied. The first was to ensure everyone got their work out and made a start on something immediately upon entering the room, almost before they could draw breath. This worked quite well, particularly if they had some work to continue from a previous lesson. Sometimes I would have some instructions already written on the board, a puzzle or a task for students to copy into their books and make a start on.

If, however, I wanted to start a new topic or to provide some fresh input, I would adopt a quite different approach. In these circumstances I would calm students as they came through the door, asking them to quietly get their books and pens out and make themselves ready to start, steadfastly though calmly refusing to answer any questions. Sometimes this could take several minutes until the last of the stragglers had entered the room. I tried to make the atmosphere calm and quiet; everything I did was aimed at promoting a controlled, composed and peaceful atmosphere. These experiences were worlds apart by comparison to other lessons with the same class at other times of the week, when students would often greet me with a friendly 'Hello' and leave at the end saying 'See you next lesson'. Yet I was the same teacher in the same room, with the same class and using the same range of teaching styles.

Expectations, classroom culture and the 3ds strategy

A different approach, which I found particularly useful, was one where I did not officially 'begin' a lesson. Instead, I signalled my expectation about students taking responsibility for getting themselves started. I felt it important for students to recognize that they were quite capable of starting work without me formally asking them. To achieve this, I would ask the first student who walked into the room to sit next to me and show me the work he or she was doing. This entailed holding a discussion based upon the following three questions: 'What have you done?' 'What are you doing?' and 'What are you going to do next?' I call this the 3ds strategy. As other students entered the room I would purposefully continue the one-to-one discussion or ask a second student to discuss their work with me. Sometimes, I would spend an entire lesson in the same vein, asking student after student to show me their work. Usually these discussions were punctuated by responding to other students' requests for help. The atmosphere was, therefore, set by the teacher already having started work, and as students entered the room they were expected to follow suit.

Talking of suits, a pack of cards can be used as a mechanism for managing a mathematics classroom with regard to some interesting problems for use in the following contexts:

- a homework task;
- to liven up a dreary lesson;
- to calm a noisy lesson;
- at the beginning of a lesson;
- at the end of a lesson;
- in a mathematics club.

The problems are all based upon a similar routine, which is a kind of 'shuffle' as follows. Turn over the top card and place it face upwards on the table. Place the next card to the bottom of the remaining pile of cards. Now repeat this sequence, the next card on top face up and the next to the bottom of the remaining pile. After several sequences all the cards will be face up on the table. The problems is to work out how to arrange the cards in the first instance so that they end up in the sequence: **A, K, A, K, A, K, A, K**. A slightly harder problem is to find how the cards were arranged to produce the sequence: **A, K, Q, A, K, Q** ...

The next task will also help students with their spelling. As each letter is spoken a card is placed at the bottom of the pile and the 'trick' proceeds as follows. Say the letter 'a' and put the top card to the bottom. Now say the letter 'c' and put the next top card to the bottom, then say 'e' and put the third card to the bottom. Turn over the next card, saying 'ace' and revealing an ACE. The puzzle is to work out the original sequence that thirteen cards must be placed in so the cards fall out as follows: '*a, c, e*' **A** '*k, i, n, g*' **K** '*q, u, e, e, n*' **Q**, **J**, **10**, **9**, **8**, **7**, **6**, **5**, **4**, **3**, **2**.

The quality of the curriculum and classroom management

My description of a card trick while in the midst of discussing classroom management issues may seem a digression. However, although many books have been written about classroom management, about styles and techniques, few link the quality of the curriculum and the use of interesting tasks with the issue of teachers developing positive approaches to classroom management. I have often heard trainee teachers being told that first of all they have to establish discipline with a class before they can try anything interesting or too risky. I argue that achieving good discipline cannot be separated from the provision of interesting tasks to work on. Sue Cowley writes about this issue in *Getting the Buggers to Behave 2* (2003, pp. 84, 91, 114). At worst, I fear that teachers who spend most of their energy establishing discipline may never get around to offering interesting tasks or using different resources. This is because they can never quite take the risk that offering interesting tasks requires, possibly because they expect the students to misbehave or misuse the resource. This creates a chicken-and-egg situation ... or do I mean a vicious circle?

Tapping into students' natural inquisitiveness

I equate interesting tasks with enquiry, with working on the human condition of wanting to know how something works. We are inquisitive creatures and in some shape or form we all solve puzzles, often for the sheer pleasure of matching our minds and our bodies against whatever form the challenge takes. We do crosswords and quizzes, play games, pose logic and lateral thinking puzzles, go orienteering, climb up rock faces and enter competitions such as 'Spot the ball' (or, if you read the *Westmorland Gazette*, 'Spot the Dog'). What motivates people to engage in such activities is the joy of solving a problem, the pleasure of pitting oneself against different types of challenges. Furthermore, a great many of the jobs people do involve problem-solving; we only have to think about how builders, plumbers, joiners and electricians go about their jobs to recognize that much of what underpins their craft is related to solving problems.

As such, problem-solving approaches to learning have significant implications on the way mathematics is taught. Causing students to pit their wits against the challenge of a problem, to engage them in thinking skills, to grab their attention and to use their brains means that concerns over managing certain adolescent behaviour become less of a focus. This is because as teachers we can shift the focus of attention away from students finding ways of winding up the teacher, towards the teacher challenging students through the problems posed. Of course, there are balances to be found: indeed, balance is everything.

Balances, continuums and soggy middles

My reference to balance is not about finding a fulcrum and sticking at that point and remaining in the soggy middle. Balancing one's teaching style is about operating at different places on a continuum, sometimes at the extremes, so that over time a balance is found. We gain much from experiencing life's contrasts. For example, I enjoy the peace and solitude, the exhilaration and the beauty of hill-walking. I also enjoy being in big crowds at football grounds, the noise and the passion, the exhilaration and the beauty of the game. Enjoyment comes not only from being in a place and soaking up its atmosphere, but is also about being able to contrast those atmospheres; the peace of the Kentmere valley and the noise of Anfield. So it is in teaching mathematics.

Here are some ways of teaching at either end of continuums.

- Asking closed questions which have specific answers and asking open questions that have more than one answer. For example: 'What are nine fours?' or 'How many ways can I multiply whole numbers together to produce an answer of 36?'
- Asking students to practise a specific skill or a routine using a structured or a less structured problem. For example, giving students a worksheet and asking them to 'Work out the areas of the shapes' or, as a more open problem, providing grid paper and asking students to 'Find all possible triangles on a 4-by-4 dot grid and work out the area of each.'
- Asking students to imagine something or giving students some practical equipment to work with. For example: 'Imagine you have four squares the same size and you are going to join them edge to edge. How many different shapes can be made?' or 'Use four square tiles to make some shapes and see how many shapes can be made using five square tiles.'
- Providing students with a specific routine to follow or asking them to come up with their own methods. For example: 'Solve some equations using the flow diagram routine' or 'Try to make up at least two of your own methods for solving equations.'
- Using different strategies when holding whole-class discussions. For example: 'Discuss with another person how you might answer the following question ...' or 'Everyone write down what you think the answer is to the following question ...'

By working in a variety of ways we are more likely to hook on to students' preferred ways of learning. One complexity of teaching is that no matter what approach or strategy we use during a particular lesson, we are not necessarily going to motivate or hold the interest of everyone. However, by actively demonstrating to students that we are capable and aware of the importance of teaching in different ways, we shall be in a strong position to form sound, professional relationships with students. Through these, together with our own relationship with mathematics, we seek to help students form confident relationships with mathematics.

'Don't smile 'til Christmas'

At the beginning of this chapter I mentioned the issue of using statements such as this. I now seek to unpick the use of such statements and consider other aspects of classroom management, such as trust and developing one's inner strength.

'Don't smile 'til Christmas'

This certainly has a grain of 'truth' insofar that disclosing certain personal details too early during encounters with a class might result in some students taking advantage of the information. At worst, the focus of a lesson will shift away from mathematics and on to more pressing concerns, such as who supports what team. In the main, however, unsmiling teachers can cause unsmiling responses from students. I have never personally been able to last more than a few minutes in a classroom before uttering some amusing comment or breaking into a smile. There's a great line from Ziggy Stardust: 'You can lick 'em by smiling.'

'Would you do that at home?'

This is a cracking line for most students to respond with 'Yes I would' or 'But I'm not at home.' Something that struck me as a young teacher was how I suddenly found myself on 'the other side', asking the rhetorical questions that I remembered my teachers had asked me as an adolescent. Such mantras didn't convince me when I was young; we can be sure future generations will remain equally unconvinced.

Developing one's inner strength

How do we find an inner strength and the confidence to face groups of 30 adolescents each day, some of whom may wish to be somewhere else, all of whom will have expectations of how a teacher ought to behave and different amounts of respect for teachers? As I wrote earlier, there are no quick fixes, no panaceas – but there are ways we can behave which might help us to feel more at ease. An 'obvious' way for me is the importance of talking to and making eye contact with students as they enter the classroom. To conclude this chapter I offer ways which have helped me find my inner strength.

Being slightly off one's trolley

Uppermost in my list of top four teaching behaviours is being ever-so-slightly crazy ... to keep students guessing whether or not I have lost my marbles, and being not quite so predictable. I have always felt that taking occasional opportunities to be overt can have an amusing impact in a lesson. For example, making a point of accentuating a mistake I have made or occasionally and purposefully falling over should I accidentally walk into something are ways of demonstrating that mistakes happen and don't always have to be covered up. Such craziness might show through the way I set up certain tasks or through the nature of a task itself. Here are a couple of tasks where I have always had a lot of fun.

The first is the Silent Function Game (SFG), an idea I first met within the pages of a fantastic though, sadly, out-of-print publication titled *Starting Points* written by Banwell, Saunders and Tahta (1972). The game is carried out in silence and therefore requires the use of mime and lots of written comments on the board. I have used this idea many times and always with enormous amounts of fun and success, including one occasion in 2001 when being observed by an inspector.

The SFG works as follows. Split the board into three vertical columns, and using three different coloured board pens (it used to be coloured chalk) title each column 'First Number', 'Second Number' and 'Comments'. The teacher then decides upon a function and writes a number in the first column (in one colour) and a number in the second column (in another colour); the second number is achieved by applying the function to the first number. The next stage is to offer the first colour of pen to a student and invite them to write a number in the first column: this might be achieved either by writing something in the 'Comment' column (in another colour pen) or miming one's intent. I apply the same function to this number and write the corresponding number in the second column. The 'Comments' section can be used to write all manner of responses; mathematically, the main intention is for students to write in words how they think the numbers in the second column are connected to those in the first column.

Through the SFG I want students to think about what is going on, to work out the function I am using and to figure out how to write the function in words and symbols. As students begin to work out what the function is I write a number in the second column and invite a volunteer to write the corresponding number in the first column. Ultimately, I want students to engage with functions and to teach without talking. By starting with simple, one operation functions and later working on functions with two operations, it is possible with some classes to introduce functions such as $n \rightarrow n^2 + n$.

A second task, which creates much mathematical mirth, is something called Logical Hats. This involves asking three volunteers to sit one in front of another with coloured hats on their heads. There are five hats altogether, three of one colour and two of another (say three red and two blue). The scenario develops as follows.

- The person at the back cannot see the colour of their own hat but can see the colours of the hats of the two people in front.
- The person in the middle can only see the colour of the hat of the person in front.
- The person at the front cannot see any hats at all.
- Each person, starting from the back, is asked: 'Do you know the colour of your hat?'
- Providing 'correct', yes/no answers are forthcoming from the back and the middle people, it is *always* possible for the person at the front to be able to work out the colour of the hat he or she is wearing.

I usually begin with the simple case and this involves placing a red hat on the person at the back and blue hats on the middle and front people. When the back person is asked the question 'Do you know the colour of your hat?' their answer has to be 'Yes'. This is because she can obviously see the only two blue hats in front. The middle person has heard the answer provided by the back person so when he is asked: 'Do you know the colour of your hat?' she/he will also be able to answer 'Yes'. Finally, the person at the front will be able to work out the colour of their hat.

The problem now develops by considering a different combination of hats. For example, with Red, Red, Blue, the person at the back must answer 'No', the person in the middle should also answer 'No' and from this information the person at the front can work out that he or she is wearing a blue hat. Asking students to prove that no matter what combination of hats are used the person at the front can always work out the colour of their hat is an interesting challenge.

After craziness, the next three in my list of preferred teaching qualities are demonstrating trust, opening doors, and finding opportunities to take 'time-outs'.

Trust

Building mutual trust with students is essential if we are to help them become evermore independent, responsible and trustworthy. Leaving the classroom in a planned, intended way is one way I demonstrate my trust of students. Of course, there are all kinds of reasons why a teacher should never leave a classroom, and rules and regulations to indicate we should not leave students unattended. Well, this might be so; but sometimes I choose to break such rules and take risks. The outcome of such actions has, in my experience, been immensely beneficial in terms of my relationships with a class. On one occasion I left a class with approximately £3,000 of graphic calculators for several minutes; this was in order to find an overhead projector, since the one in my room had been 'borrowed' by a colleague. On another occasion I didn't arrive at a class until 20 minutes into the lesson: the story goes as follows.

It was that time in the school calendar when Year 11 students were to have their final day in school before leaving for the examination period. I was a Year 11 form tutor and had been with the class for four years. On the Friday morning there was due to be a leaving assembly, and because I was a tutor I would be in attendance. I was fairly confident the assembly would run over into Period, 1 which was when I had a Year 7 class to teach. As it happened, I was also expecting a group of mathematics teachers from schools in a nearby town to visit the department to observe mixed-ability mathematics teaching.

Anticipating this set of circumstances, I explained to my Year 7 class during registration prior to Period 1 that I would probably be late, and established they knew what they were doing and where all the equipment was they would need. At the end of the previous lesson we had begun to make posters about the work they had been doing, and I had allocated this lesson for students to complete their posters. I explained some visitors would be arriving and asked the class to make them feel welcome, to show them what they were doing and to answer any questions the visitors might have. So Friday Period 1 arrived, and the assembly runs over by five, ten, fifteen minutes. By the time I get to my Year 7 class I am almost 20 minutes late. Inside the room there is a hive of activity and the visitors are engaged in various conversations with students. I am greeted with a few 'hellos' and so the lesson progresses.

At the end of the day I met with the visitors to discuss what they made of their visit. What I had not expected was their disbelief at what had occurred in Period 1 – at the fact that the class had been able to get on with their work, that students had been able to get equipment out and not throw it around the classroom, and all without their teacher being there. I found this immensely interesting because I had not for one moment expected the class to do anything other than get themselves started and settle to their tasks; this was, after all, how we had come to understand what our mathematics classroom was all about. Over the year we had built up the trust that was so fundamental to their development.

Opening doors

I heard a marvellous anecdote a few years ago told to me by a parent who had attended an evening for children moving from their primary schools to a secondary school: the headteacher is welcoming parents and talking about life at the school. He begins by talking about expectations and respect and gives an example that if he is walking down a corridor he expects students to open doors for him. (Quiet mutters from some parents in agreement that children should respect their elders.) 'If, however, I get to a door first then I expect to open the door for a student!' There are issues here of respect being based not upon position or authority, age or seniority, but upon mutuality. This anecdote resonates with teaching mathematics, about the teacher opening doors for students, about finding ways of helping students open doors for themselves and for each other. Opening doors in a mathematics classroom is about integrity, about treating students with dignity and offering them access to mathematics.

Taking time-outs

A powerful classroom management strategy is to take time-outs – creating time during a lesson to actively do nothing. Classrooms are incredibly busy places, and as teachers we can all too easily find ourselves in a continual state of doing, talking, responding, organizing and conducting. In each lesson we make dozens of decisions, mostly in the moment; before we have completed one interaction we become aware our attention is required elsewhere in the classroom. Making so many decisions about what to say, how to say it, when to say something, when not to say something, whether to answer one student's question or ask another question instead is just what teaching is fundamentally about.

Taking a time-out provides opportunities for students to be more self-reliant. Asking one student to help another, or explain to another what to do next, are important ways of temporarily having another 'teacher' in the classroom; students also enhance their understanding when they explain something to another person. Because classrooms are so busy it is important to create time when we stop all this 'doing' and take a time-out, perhaps standing at the back of the room and surveying the scene. To do nothing, just for a minute or two, to observe what is happening, to marvel at how well a lesson is going, to say to ourselves what bloody good teachers we are, to congratulate ourselves on doing such a wonderful job, is an essential part of managing any classroom.

12

DEVELOPING
STUDENTS'
THINKING
SKILLS

One traditional view of teaching is of 'passing on' knowledge. When asked the question 'Why do you want to teach?' I have heard many prospective teachers respond: 'Because I want to pass on my knowledge.' This may appear a perfectly reasonable thing to want to do – after all, we have had someone else's knowledge passed on to us; but it does however raise two issues. The first is whether one's knowledge is worth 'passing on'; if all that each generation ever learnt was knowledge passed on by a previous generation, then we would find ourselves in an ever-decreasing knowledge spiral. This, of course, is the complete opposite of what does happen; the knowledge base across the planet has increased at what appears to be an amazing rate. The second issue is that if future generations are going to learn more than the current generation can possibly know, what roles do teachers play in this process? What part does a mathematics teacher play in facilitating the possibility of and creating the conditions for some students going well beyond that teacher's mathematical knowledge base?

There currently is a deal of energy being put into the teaching of thinking skills, and this is connected to developments such as 'Philosophy for children' (P4C). In this chapter I explore how such initiatives can naturally fit into mathematics classrooms, and in doing so offer the notion that teaching is far, far more than passing on knowledge.

Teaching thinking skills in mathematics classrooms

Whether it is possible to *teach* thinking skills is worth considera-tion. I cannot teach another person to think because I do not have sufficient knowledge of neurology, about how the brain works. I cannot begin, therefore, to know how thinking can be taught. However, I can construct environments where students can learn to deepen and sharpen their thinking skills. I seek to achieve this by teaching through questioning, by which I mean asking non-rhetorical, open questions. Before going any further it will be useful to define what thinking skills are and how they connect with mathematics.

So, what are thinking skills?

There is a great risk of boring the reader by presenting a list of process skills such as *simplifying, systematizing, conjecturing, predicting, generalizing* and so on, which only come to life when there are problems to be solved. Without contexts and problems through which these skills can emerge, they are merely platitudes. We must consider the kind of problems we offer within mathematics classrooms and the kind of strategies and tasks that might help students develop their thinking. The development of such skills is only a starting point; thinking skills must be transferable not just across the mathematics curriculum, but across the entire curriculum.

With this in mind it is inappropriate to plan a scheme of work where thinking skills are dealt with in isolation. For example, having separate 'thinking skills' lessons may seem to suggest that in other lessons thinking is not the central intention! Therefore, to enhance students' learning, thinking skills need to be integrated within and developed throughout the entire curriculum: this is the same with regard to P4C. Encouraging students to think deeply about something, to consider alternatives, to view something from another person's perspective, to ask 'What if?' and 'Why?' type questions are at the root of learning and developing socially, emotionally and rationally.

The following suggestions are ideas that have at their core the development of thinking skills to help students make sense of the underlying mathematics. The remainder of this chapter is, therefore, set out in three sections:

- making sense of conventions and unravelling vocabulary;
- exploring systems and structures;
- classifying, grouping, ordering and naming.

Making sense of conventions and unravelling vocabulary

One of the 'questions' young children often ask and frequently turn into a repetitive questioning game is 'Why?' Once a child has hooked an adult into playing the 'Why, why, why?' game, there is obviously a lot of fun being had. Asking 'why' questions is probably the most potent way of trying to make sense of mathematics and to go deeper into a problem. Making sense of mathematics involves knowing the conventions associated with concepts and understanding the vocabulary used to describe and to discuss mathematics. Vocabulary and symbols are gateways to making sense of mathematics. If we cannot understand the vocabulary or if the symbols are meaningless hieroglyphics then mathematics is likely to become inaccessible, obscure and mysterious.

Taking all opportunities to make sense of conventions and unravel associated vocabulary is therefore of enormous importance. Such opportunities need to be created and, by setting up problem-solving situations where students are encouraged to ask 'why' questions, to work within appropriate contexts and to be explicit about associated vocabulary, is fundamental to understanding. When learners understand why something works and when they have access to vocabulary, when they feel a part of what is going on, when they are included, they not only become more effective learners, there is increased motivation, increased self-esteem, better behaved classes ... *everything is connected.*

The following ideas are based upon an exploration of coordinates and transformations. Plotting points on a grid using the convention of coordinates is a defined system: a horizontal shift followed by a vertical shift. Students need to make sense of why the convention is important; creating opportunities to explore this convention is essential if they are to appreciate its significance. One strategy is to ask students to plot the coordinates of a shape both the 'right' and the 'wrong' way round so two (congruent) shapes are produced, one being a reflection of the other in the $y = x$ line.

Already a situation ripe for discussion exists, not for students to decide which is the best way to plot coordinates, but for them to know there is a recognized convention to enable consistent communication between *shape-plotters*. Of course, the teacher could set up a discussion about the value of and the need for any convention. Indeed, holding a discussion about what other conventions exist in mathematics (for example, order of operations and the need for them) can be valuable.

In terms of helping students to engage with vocabulary such as horizontal and vertical shifts and the associated symbols x and y, there is always a balance between using the 'correct' notation and the possibility of students being 'ready' to embrace the ideas. Some people argue that the accepted vocabulary and symbols should be used at the outset, to prevent students having to 'unlearn' what they may have earlier been taught. Others would argue that fastidiousness to detail forms barriers to understanding. What seems important here is the sensitivity of the teacher and the decisions they purposefully make to promote students' understanding. For instance, whether to label axes h and v for horizontal and vertical in the first instance and to offer x and y as the accepted convention later. The key issue is providing contexts within which such discussions can take place.

Exploring systems and structures

If making sense of conventions relates to 'why' questions, exploring systems and structures is about asking 'how' and 'what' questions. Knowing *how* a system works and *what* happens when conditions are altered or when parameters are changed (by applying some kind of rule) underpins understanding.

By working with the convention of plotting points on a two-dimensional grid, students can explore the structure of coordinates through transformations, and this will involve an investigation of shapes in all four quadrants. Asking students to consider what happens when certain rules are applied to the coordinates that define the corners of a simple shape can help such an exploration develop. My preference is to ask students to begin with an asymmetrical quadrilateral, drawn in the first quadrant, and to record the coordinates of the corners of the shape. Some rules and subsequent transformations are:

Rule	Transformation
Add a constant to each pair of ordinates	Vector translation
Add or subtract different constants to each x and y ordinate	Vector translation
Double the size of each ordinate	Enlargement by a factor of 2 with the centre of enlargement at the origin
Keep the x ordinate the same and make the y ordinate negative	Reflection in $y = 0$
Make each x ordinate negative and keep each y ordinate the same	Reflection in $x = 0$
Make both ordinates negative	A rotation of $180°$ about $(0, 0)$
Swap the ordinates around and make the 'new' x ordinate negative	Anti-clockwise rotation of $90°$ about $(0, 0)$
Add 1 to the x ordinate then multiply by 2, add 3 to the y ordinate then multiply by 2	Enlargement by a factor of 2 from the centre $(^-2, ^-6)$

Here students are exploring the system of transformations on a coordinate grid, and while I have provided some rules in the examples above, students can equally construct rules themselves and try to make sense of the outcomes.

Such an exploration would provide challenging starting points for a Year 7 or a Year 10 class, depending upon the complexity of the initial rules suggested. If the same idea is used with undergraduates they will only be a short hop from developing concepts of transformations by matrices, and another from group theory. Such is the power of using tasks through which students can explore structures and systems and simultaneously engage in ever-more complex concepts. Software such as Omnigraph can also be used to produce transformations, and such a resource can further enhance students' thinking skills.

Classifying, grouping, ordering and naming

To classify something we need to see what similarities and differences exist between objects under consideration. Classifying is essentially a sorting exercise based upon certain properties. Geometry provides many contexts for students to develop ideas of classifying, grouping, ordering and naming. A sequence of lessons I have used on several occasions is based upon classifying shapes using Geo-strips. These are coloured plastic strips with small holes that can be joined together with split-pins. The first lesson takes some organizing: however, I have always found the quality of discussion which ensues is worth the extra effort required in setting up the task.

In small groups I provide students with nine strips, three long strips (**L**), three middle-length strips (**M**) and three short strips (**S**). Each group is given different lengths of strips. This is because I want groups to make different numbers of triangles from the collection of strips with which they are provided.

Students are asked to make as many different triangles as possible, each time using just three strips and clipping them together by the holes at each end. They code each triangle using combinations of the symbols **L**, **M** and **S**. Some groups will be able to make the maximum of ten possible triangles with the following codes: **LLL, MMM, SSS, LLM, LLS, MML, MMS, SSL, SSM** and **LMS**. Other groups will only be able to make a subset of these ten triangles, and this will depend upon the relative lengths of **L**, **M** and **S**. So if the lengths of **S** + **M** $\leqslant$ **L**, or if 2**M** $\leqslant$ **L**, or if 2**S** $\leqslant$ **M**, shorter lists are possible. The intention is to engage students with conditions for making triangles according to the lengths of the sides by entering into a discussion about why some groups have been able to make ten triangles whereas others have made fewer.

The key factor here is for students to engage with ambiguity, to try to sort out why something occurs as it does. Opportunities to name the shapes and use vocabulary of congruence and similarity will be a possibility. This is a starting point for a much more complex exploration of what happens when we use four strips and make quadrilaterals. Because of the loss of rigid structure when using just three strips, the possibility of making an infinite number of quadrilaterals using four strips emerges. This 'forces' students to organize and classify information.

The next stage is to consider what parameters affect the ways quadrilaterals can be classified. What follows will certainly appear to be a staged set of instructions and may appear to run counter to the notion of students developing thinking skills. However, my intention here is to offer a structure within which many questions can be asked and students can develop their understanding of classifying at different rates according to how far they are able to develop the ideas offered. (At this point I would like to acknowledge Eric Love, my former Head of Mathematics at Wyndham School, Egremont, who first presented the idea to me in 1975.)

Once some quadrilaterals have been made and the issue of an infinite number of shapes has been established, the notion of classifying according to properties can be discussed. Finding the balance between how much the teacher guides and how much the teacher stands back to enable students to form conclusions is a key issue.

One approach is to ask students to discuss the properties of parallel sides (*Pops*) and the number of right angles (*RAs*) that quadrilaterals can possibly have. The idea develops by students finding quadrilaterals with pairs of properties formed from 0, 1 or 2 *Pops* combined with 0, 1, 2 or 4 *RAs*. As it happens, from these twelve pairs of combinations only seven essentially different quadrilaterals can be formed:

Pops	RAs	*Possible* quadrilateral
0	0	An asymmetric quadrilateral or a kite
0	1	An asymmetric quadrilateral or a kite
0	2	A kite
1	0	An isosceles and/or an asymmetric trapezium
1	2	An asymmetric trapezium
2	0	A parallelogram
2	4	A rectangle

The next and most complex aspect of this sequence of ideas is to introduce a third property: the number of equal sides (*ES*) any shape can have. There are five such possibilities: shapes with 0, 2, 3, 4 or two pairs of equal sides. By combining these five possibilities with the seven from the table above, there are 35 pairs; the challenge is to find which of these 35 combinations of properties produce quadrilaterals.

Throughout this sequence of tasks students have opportunities to work with properties of shapes and name and classify them accordingly. There will be much scope to discuss the vocabulary associated with quadrilaterals and work on issues such as why a square is a rectangle and similarly a rhombus and a parallelogram. There are massive opportunities here for students to use drawing implements to construct shapes and use dynamic geometry software to create shapes.

This exploration provides the most confident 13 or 14-year-old mathematician with significant stimulation. Furthermore, because the task is accessible and equipment-rich, all students will have opportunities to develop their mathematical thinking, irrespective of their so-called 'level' of attainment.

Integrating thinking skills into mainstream mathematics lessons

At the beginning of this chapter I mentioned the issue of integrating thinking skills into the curriculum. To achieve this, investigative methods of learning need to be encouraged as a 'normal' way of teaching. This can be achieved by setting up explorations of concepts using 'simple' and 'accessible' tasks. Before looking at some of these I offer a brief historical perspective of how investigative ways of working have been misconstrued as the act of 'doing an investigation'.

Since the Cockcroft report in 1982, and the advent of coursework in mainstream mathematics classrooms through GCSE from 1986, there has been a growth in students 'doing investigations'. These have been characterized through problems such as *Frogs Max Box* and a plethora of other investigations, many of which ended up with certain sequences of numbers, typically 1, 3, 6, 10, 15 ... and 1, 2, 3, 5, 8, 13 ... Such problems are frequently a bolt-on type of experience where students are guided towards producing and generalizing sequences.

Because such problems become the vehicle for assessment of coursework, GCSE students are often taught the rules of the game:

- simplify the problem;
- collect results;
- put them into a table;
- write about any patterns noticed;
- produce a formula or general result.

This approach has become an algorithmic process and, through the institutionalization of investigation work, problem-solving has been subjugated to the necessity of passing a test. As such, this approach bears little resemblance to the reality of trying to solve a problem where 'stuckness' and messiness often emerge. Offering problems where students have to think about something in depth, make decisions about how to proceed, consider what parameters might be changed, explore different avenues and not feel downhearted if they are unable to find a complete solution creates a more realistic view of mathematics.

In order to integrate thinking skills into the mathematics curriculum, students need to be offered a wide range of problem-solving opportunities from the youngest possible age. In the secondary school I advocate that the first lesson should be about solving a problem, so students gain a sense of what learning mathematics in their new school is about. Subsequent lessons can all have elements of puzzling and problem-solving so that thinking skills become a natural feature of lessons. Problems need to provide opportunities for students to manipulate parameters, order information, discuss different solutions and, wherever possible, prove something, perhaps in relation to having gained a complete set of results. Problems might begin from a specific, reasonably closed statement yet have in-built opportunities for extension. For example:

1. *How many ways can the number 5 be partitioned by addition?* This could be developed by looking at partitions of other numbers and, in turn, lead to an exploration of Pascal's Triangle (if, for example, 1 + 1 + 3 and 1 + 3 + 1 are counted as different partitions).

2. *Using the digits 1, 2, 3 and 4 and one multiplication sign, what are the largest and smallest answers that can be found?* (For example, 12 × 34, 231 × 4 etc.) This could lead to students producing a systematic list in order to find all possible answers.

3. *How many shapes can be made on a 3-by-3, 9-dot grid?* This could become an exploration of area and be developed by extending the grid size. Not far away could be some work on Pick's Theorem, where the area of a shape can be calculated by knowing the number of dots on the perimeter and the number of dots inside a shape.

4. *How many different rectangles can be made with an area of 20 square units?* This could lead to work on pairs of factors and be developed into work on fractions and decimals (for example, $2\frac{1}{2}$ by 8, 3.2 by 6.25), square roots (for example, finding the length of a square with area 20), and, because $20 = 2^2 + 4^2$, Pythagoras could also be on the cards.

5. *What does the graph of multiples of 2 look like?* This could lead to work on graphing and comparing other sets of multiples, including multiples of a $\frac{1}{2}$. What about a graph of one more than the multiples of 2 or two less than the multiples of 3?

6. *What is the median height of the class?* This could lead to finding and comparing the median heights of other classes, perhaps

to calculate what the average percentage height increase is across each year group.

The pleasure of teaching mathematics in ways that cause learners to use and develop thinking skills while working on content skills is grounded in a holistic vision of learning and a heuristic view of mathematics. There are oodles of opportunities to take the simplest of tasks and extend them into more complex areas. Finding ways of extending 'simple', 'rich' starting points so students can work on different levels of complexity and ultimately become capable of going beyond producing 'quick' answers to closed questions is not just interesting and good fun: it is absolutely essential.

13

TEACHING
MATHEMATICS
WITHOUT A
TEXTBOOK

Call it vandalism, but those old textbooks had it coming and were destined for the bin anyway. I had been teaching for just a few weeks in my new role as Head of Mathematics and had set myself a target of seeing how long I could sustain teaching without using a textbook. I'd arrived from my previous school with a lot of experience of teaching mathematics using investigative approaches based upon a 'modular' structure, where topics would run for two to three weeks, and assessment at 16+ had a 40 per cent coursework weighting. I intuitively believed problem-solving was the most interesting and valuable way for children to learn mathematics, and I wanted to develop this way of working in my new department.

Three weeks into the job I decided to offer my Year 9 class the Möbius Band problem, an idea I had used before (I am sure most mathematics teachers will have met the Möbius Band before, but just in case anybody has not: it is a strip of paper with a half twist put into it and joined end to end). Recycling old textbooks to generate the required strips of paper seemed a better option than using pristine A4 paper, and while students cut strips of paper from the torn out pages of the textbooks I speedily dispensed sellotape to each group.

The task is to explore what happens when the following process is carried out:

1. Put one, two, and three half twists into three different strips of paper.
2. Sellotape the ends of each strip together to form Möbius bands.
3. Cut lengthways through the middle of each joined-up strip, following the curve of each band, until something happens.

A demonstration of what happens after one twist and one cut, followed by a second cut, makes for an enjoyable and intriguing start to a lesson, particularly if students are asked to predict what they think will happen before each cut is completed. An interesting result which I had not met before was when one student ended up with one small strip and one large strip linked together after 'one' cut down the 'middle' from a band containing one half twist. Well, it is not exactly 'one' cut and not exactly through the 'middle', but if you haven't come across this solution before you may wish to explore how it's done.

So, what were the students learning? On the cognitive side they were learning about degrees of turn, about how to classify and how to record the outcomes. They were learning about the importance of recording results systematically and seeing how to make sense of what happened. They were learning how to describe the outcomes using mathematical vocabulary. They were solving a problem and making predictions. On the affective side they were learning that mathematics can be enjoyable, to be careful and patient and that they were all capable of making a start on the task. At the end of the lesson, some turned themselves into kings and queens by adorning their heads with Möbius Bands: given this was the last lesson of the day and their excitement would not need to be quelled by a colleague, I felt comfortable with this outcome. They were also learning that mathematics did not need to reside in the pages of a textbook or the teacher's head; active, practical tasks can be part of mathematics lessons.

I learnt that if I had enough starter tasks I could provide students with access to the entire mathematics curriculum, specifically by teaching in a problem-posing, problem-solving manner. What I needed were tasks that everyone could do, and that could be extended for students who worked at different speeds and for those who engaged with mathematics at different depths of understanding. I now turn to some reasons for not using a textbook.

Who or what controls my teaching?

If one of the main purposes of a textbook is to allow students to practise a skill and consolidate knowledge, I am interested in how I can cause students to achieve the same outcome – but using different strategies and approaches. One of the difficulties with textbooks is that they allow authors to invade our classrooms, giving problems to children they obviously do not

know and making assumptions about individual student progression which they cannot possibly make; this progression is
usually set out in a chapter-by-chapter, exercise-by-exercise
approach. Yet why should I relinquish responsibility for
progression and structure to another person when I know
nothing of the pedagogy upon which they attempt to order my
students' learning?

Real-life contrivance

Further reasons for not using a textbook relate to 'real-life'
contexts. As sources of 'real-life', textbooks are out of date the
moment they are bought. Furthermore, there is an absence of
references to 'real' local sources, and any chapter based upon
real-life information is likely to be a contrivance and largely
irrelevant to adolescents' lives. For example, chapters on algebra
often suggest that plumbers and electricians work out what they
are going to charge customers according to certain formulae. This
is clearly not the case and so students are not only being
misinformed about real-life situations, they are also being
provided with a disingenuous perspective on the uses of
mathematics.

Student ownership of learning

The importance of ownership is that students are able to claim
some control over what and how they learn. However, questions
in textbooks are mostly closed and inevitably rhetorical; the same
page-by-page path has been trodden by many students of
previous generations. The implications of this is to undermine
ownership, stifle creativity and provide students with unim-
aginative ways of learning mathematics.

Strategies beyond a textbook

Although teaching with a textbook does not prevent the
construction and use of a number of alternative strategies, using
a textbook as the main resource does not help create the

conditions or the need for developing a wide range of strategies to be used as appropriate. Of course, it is the teacher who must judge what 'appropriate' means within the context of his or her classroom, and determine what kinds of strategies are worth using. An over-emphasis on textbook use can create a dependency both for teachers and students. For teachers, we can all too easily get seduced into asking students to work through exercises which, in the main, requires the use of a limited strategy. This strategy involves working through some examples similar to questions in the textbook and asking students to 'Turn to page 27 and do exercise A' – possibly with extension questions on page 28. There is an important issue here about developing teacher professionalism. Working without a textbook creates the possibility of devising and using a wider range of teaching strategies. This, in turn, promotes greater creativity and more imaginative ways of teaching, fostering the conditions in which more interesting classroom activities and more effective forms of learning can occur.

Student dependence on textbooks

For students, an over-dependence upon textbooks can result in them believing that mathematics is predominantly about getting right or wrong answers, and success is measured by the number of ticks they receive, either from the teacher or themselves when answers to exercises are read out. The dangers of students working in such ways are ubiquitous. Conversely, providing more open-ended types of situations results in students developing abilities to think something through and use a range of problem-solving strategies.

In the remainder of this chapter I consider a range of strategies to support the teaching and learning of mathematics. The first focuses on ways to encourage students to develop concepts and practise and consolidate skills.

Practise and consolidation

There are hundreds of problems and situations that can be set up for students to work on and, as a consequence, enable them to practise skills and consolidate their understanding of concepts. I offer two contexts. The first is based upon using a 9-pin geoboard. This is a piece of equipment made from a block of wood and nine nails arranged in a 3-by-3 square. The size of the board is in the region of 15 to 20cm square; over time I have made dozens of these. More recently I made some with 15mm Escutcheon pins. These are bright golden nails with round heads and produce the most beautiful finished items.

The 9-pin geoboard is possibly the most remarkable piece of equipment for providing students with access to a wide range of mathematics and for providing the teacher with the potential for generating an amazing amount of ideas. It is a 'closed' environment from which many 'open' problems can arise. The power of the 9-pin geoboard lies in its simplicity – and the fact that it can be made from scrap wood, a lick of paint, a hammer and a few nails.

Generating problems on a 9-pin Geoboard

One strategy I find useful is to give out the equipment and grid paper and seemingly 'ignore' students' questions for the next few minutes. My experience is that students usually begin to work with the equipment, and while I pretend not to hear questions such as 'What are we supposed to be doing?' I am watchful over what is happening. Experience tells me that students naturally begin to interact with the equipment, often working together, and they soon start to make shapes and formulate questions.

After a few minutes of relatively free play, I ask them what they have been doing and these responses typically occur:

- 'I've been trying to make all the numbers from 1 to 9.'
- 'I have been trying to make the letters of the alphabet.'
- 'We've been making star shapes.'

- 'I made a shape and my friend tried to make a reflection of the shape.'
- 'I've been making triangles.'
- 'I have been making shapes that don't touch the middle pin.'

Because somebody always says something about making different shapes, I build upon such a contribution by asking students to make and record shapes, and so the first problem emerges; to find all the possible quadrilaterals. Again, here is the issue of ownership of the problem growing from an idea students have begun to think about. Ownership is important so that students feel they have some input into the direction a lesson takes.

I usually choose to pose the problem of finding all the different quadrilaterals slightly ambiguously in terms of whether rotations, reflections or translations 'count' as being different. These are key concepts I want to develop during a whole-class discussion later in the lesson. To initiate discussion I ask individuals to come to the board and draw one of their shapes on the 20 or so 9-dot grids I have previously drawn on the board. If I have not had time to prepare the board before the lesson, I use my deftly honed skill of speedily drawing grids as students are working on their quadrilateral-finding task. This is typical of the competencies teachers develop under pressure! Alternatively, I can pass around an overhead transparency with a number of 9 dot grids printed on it along with an OHP pen, and ask students to record their shapes on this.

Once we have a board/screen full of contributions, an open question about what anyone notices about the shapes inevitably provokes discussion about which shapes are the same or different. I ascribe each individual grid/shape a letter of the alphabet, thus enabling identification when comments such as 'Shape C is the same as shape M' are made.

Asking students to justify their observations opens up opportunities to develop concepts of congruence and similarity. In turn, I can promote the use of vocabulary such as rotation, reflection and translation and enlargement. I will certainly guide discussion towards the properties of the shapes, in terms of equal length of sides, parallel sides and right angles. This leads to naming and classifying the shapes. The issue of recording vocabulary and listing key words is an aspect of making terminology explicit, usually followed up with a discussion about the meaning of certain words. A valuable piece of equipment to have is a plastic transparent 9-pin geoboard. This means shapes can be projected onto a screen and can be utilized to discuss rotations and reflections of shapes.

As discussion develops, I rub out congruent shapes until we are left with a set of non-congruent quadrilaterals. Often a student will draw a triangle with a 'leg' hanging off a side or a corner. If this occurs, I have an excellent opportunity to unpick a misconception about what constitutes a quadrilateral. If no such shape appears I will add one to the collection to ensure we have a discussion about what defines a quadrilateral. Another shape that frequently appears is a 'crossed quadrilateral'. This can provide a useful focal point to discuss the differences between a 'normal' quadrilateral and one that has been drawn with four straight edges but, by crossing over, has produced two triangles joined at a point. An extension task, to find and classify all the crossed quadrilaterals, provides a suitable challenge for some students.

Properties and names of shapes, angle, area and perimeter

If all 16 possible quadrilaterals have not been found, this could be the task for the next part of a lesson. I will certainly ask students to name each quadrilateral they draw. Other tasks based upon the shapes found could be:

- Determine the symmetries of each shape.
- Draw shapes on enlarged grids so students can measure the angles with a protractor.
- Work out the area of each shape (I establish first that the area of the 1-by-1 square is one square unit).
- Find how many congruent shapes there are for each quadrilateral.
- Find the perimeter of each shape; there are three ways this might be done:

a)   by measuring;
b)   by algebraic coding (see diagram below); and, for post-Pythagoreans,
c)   by writing the perimeter in surd form (I develop this later in the chapter).

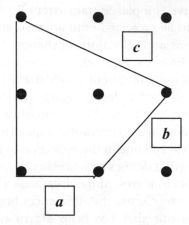

Students can write the perimeter of each shape by using the different lengths a, b, and c. Furthermore, they have a purposeful context for collecting like terms: thus, the shape above has a perimeter of $3a + b + c$.

As well as finding all the possible quadrilaterals, students might be given the problem of finding all the possible triangles on a 9-dot grid, and devising a systematic method to try to prove they have found them all. The triangle problem can be extended to find all the triangles on a 16-dot grid, so any systematic method students may devise for a 9-dot grid can be adapted to a 16-dot grid. There also exists the possibility, as the grid size increases, to work on the idea that triangles with the same base and between the same pair of parallel lines have the same area, and to connect this to the standard formula for the area of a triangle: $A = \frac{1}{2}\,bh$.

Every time a student measures an angle, calculates an area or describes a perimeter, they are naturally carrying out repetitive actions, and this is the basis of practice and consolidation. Yet no textbook is required, as each calculation arises from the work students are already involved in. All that is needed is an accessible, 'rich' problem to be posed by the teacher or, even better, for students to construct a problem for themselves.

So far, the ideas generated by using a 9-pin geoboard have been typically within the domain of lower school curriculum. However, this piece of equipment can also be used as a starting point for students to practise more complex concepts such as Pythagoras, surds, rounding, vectors, trigonometry and equations of straight lines, as described below.

Pythagoras, surds, rounding, vectors, trigonometry and equations of straight lines

There are five different lengths on a 9-dot board (1, 2, $\sqrt{2}$, $2\sqrt{2}$ and $\sqrt{5}$), and post-Pythagorean students can practise their knowledge of surds, writing the length of each side and summing these to find the perimeter of each shape made. This idea can easily be developed so that instead of leaving answers in surd form, students could be asked to calculate the perimeters of each shape to one decimal place. Such a task provides opportunities to deal with issues of premature rounding and using the shape above. On page 195 both results of 6.6 and 6.7 might be produced, but only one is, of course, correct.

For students to develop their understanding of concepts of trigonometry, vectors and equations of straight lines, the following questions might be posed:

- What size are the angles for each quadrilateral made on a 9-dot grid? Students can practise trigonometry by calculating each angle to one decimal place.
- How many different vectors are there on a 9-pin geoboard? This can be developed to consider how many vectors there are on 16, 25, 36 ... dot grids. The problem can lead students to make a systematic collection to try to find all possible results. Such a task also creates the opportunity for students to recognize that for every vector there is another equal and opposite vector created by changing the polarity of the elements. Furthermore, there is a quadratic sequence to be found, connecting the size of the board with the total number

191

of vectors. This provides students with an in-context problem for writing the *n*th term of the sequence produced.

- How many pairs of vectors that are perpendicular to each other can be made on a 9 or a 16-pin geoboard?
- What happens to the elements of a vector when it is rotated through 90°?
- By turning the geoboard grid into a coordinate grid, how many different straight lines are there and what is the equation of each one? This is another good problem, particularly as there are 20 different equations of lines to be found, and by extending the problem to a 16-dot grid, there are between 50 and 60 solutions. There is also an interesting connection between this and the earlier problem about how many vectors there are on a 9-dot grid.
- Finding the area of shapes whose vertices are not always on a pin will provide a suitable challenge for the higher attaining students; two such problems are:
  a) calculating the intersecting area made when two triangles cross over;
  b) calculating the area of a crossed quadrilateral.

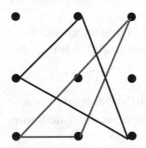 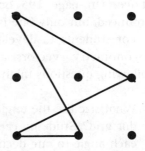

Seeking solutions to these final two problems will require students to draw upon a wide range of skills such as coordinates, equations of lines, solving simultaneous equations, working out the distance between two points, applying the cosine rule and calculating the area of a triangle. Further questions can be constructed continually, and as each one is worked on there exist possibilities for students to practise, consolidate and develop their mathematics.

This wealth of mathematics for students to engage with has all been based upon a simple grid, some starting-point questions and some development tasks, with not a textbook in sight. We have not even begun to explore some of the problems arising from a 3-by 3-by-3 dot three-dimensional grid, such as how many 3D vectors there are and what cube dissections are possible. However, I feel it is time to leave geoboards and consider another area of the curriculum that students can work on without a textbook: setting up and solving simultaneous equations.

Setting up and solving simultaneous equations

One way of solving a pair of simultaneous equations is to set up a task where each student begins by knowing what the solutions for x and y are when written as a coordinate pair. The process can be constructed as follows:

1. Each student thinks of a pair of coordinates, e.g. (**3, 11**)
2. He or she then makes up two calculations where **3** is transformed into **11**, for example $4 \times \mathbf{3} - 1 = \mathbf{11}$ and $2 \times \mathbf{3} + 5 = \mathbf{11}$.
3. Now each calculation is turned into an equation where the **3** is replaced by x and the **11** is replaced by y, for example $4x - 1 = \mathbf{y}$ and $2x + 5 = \mathbf{y}$.
4. Students give their pairs of equations to one another. In order for the 'swap-over' to happen 'simultaneously', the class can be set a time limit for producing pairs of equations.
5. Students have to try to work out the values for **x** and **y** for each pair of equations they have received.
6. Students subsequently check each other's answers.

There is a likelihood that students will use trial and improvement to work out the unknown values: in the first instance this is fine. What is important is to understand that when equations are solved simultaneously, one mental model is to see the solution as a point on a coordinate grid. Whether the teacher suggests other methods for reaching a solution or asks students to invent their own methods is, of course, a decision for individual teachers to make. Some may suggest a graphical approach, while others may turn a pair of equations into a single equation, so using the above example students can try to solve:

$$4x - 1 = 2x + 5$$

This strategy combines three different ways for students to work: in pairs, individually and discussing ideas and methods in the whole group. The next idea is based initially upon students working as a pair; the mathematical content is working with fractions. The only resource required is some brightly coloured paper cut into A5 size.

Adding and subtracting fractions

Providing students with opportunities to work as a pair, in order to discuss an idea or solve a problem jointly, is a strategy that can be used purposefully and to good effect with many tasks in a mathematics classroom. Sharing ideas to discuss something or combining information is a powerful way of enabling deeper study of a concept. To illustrate this, I offer a paired task that focuses on adding, subtracting and dividing fractions, carried out through paper-folding.

Each student is given a piece of A5 paper and asked to fold it into thirds across the short side and into quarters across the long side (A4 paper is also fine, but twice the price). This will produce twelve twelfths:

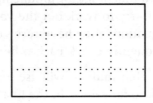

Holding a discussion about what happens, what size the individual pieces are and how they relate to the folds may be useful at this juncture. Asking students to confirm that thirds and quarters can be expressed as a number of twelfths is central to the next task. (What happens in any individual teacher's classroom, the decisions teachers make about how to intervene, and the nature of such interventions, are not what this or any other author has the authority to determine. As such, the ideas are suggestions that others may wish to weave into their practice. The ideas certainly do not require any textbooks.)

The next task is to ask student to fold their piece of paper into $\frac{2}{3}$ of the original size and their partner to fold their piece into $\frac{3}{4}$ of the original size. Now comes the crux of the problem. I ask pairs of students to add their fractional pieces of paper together:

$$\frac{2}{3} + \frac{3}{4}$$

Using the two pieces of paper we have:

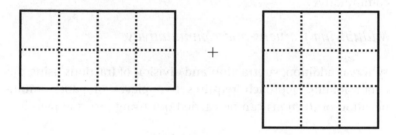

or $\frac{8}{12} + \frac{9}{12}$

Given the student holding the $\frac{2}{3}$ size will automatically have $\frac{8}{12}$ and the student with the $\frac{3}{4}$ will have $\frac{9}{12}$, the answer $\frac{17}{12}$ cannot be too far away from being realized.

The same type of process can be used for carrying out subtraction, so $\frac{3}{4} - \frac{2}{3}$ becomes $\frac{9}{12} - \frac{8}{12}$, producing the required answer of $\frac{1}{12}$.

While I do not claim that all students will automatically understand what is going on here, such a demonstration does open up the opportunity for discussion and exploration. Asking students to add other pairs of fractions involving thirds and quarters, thirds and fifths and so on will provide students with more practice of adding and subtracting fractions.

Dividing fractions and non-commutativity

To carry out a computation of $\frac{3}{4} \div \frac{2}{3}$, 'all' we have to do is to place the $\frac{3}{4}$ piece 'above' a division line and the $\frac{2}{3}$ piece 'below' it. This might be enacted in a physical sense by asking one student to lend an arm, held out horizontally, and defining this as the division line. One student then holds the $\frac{9}{12}$ above and the other holds the $\frac{8}{12}$ piece below the division line. Using the folded pieces of paper we physically produce a situation with pieces of paper containing 9 (twelfths) over (divided by) 8 (twelfths), so producing the required answer of $\frac{9}{8}$. By inverting the calculation the answer of $\frac{8}{9}$ will be achieved, and this may enable students to recognize that the process of division of fractions is not commutative.

Multiplying fractions and commutativity

Whereas addition, subtraction and division of fractions using this paper folding approach requires two pieces of paper, multiplication of fractions can be carried out using just one piece:

- Take a piece of paper that has been folded into twelve twelfths.
- Fold this into three-quarters of the original size.
- Now fold this piece into two thirds of its present size.

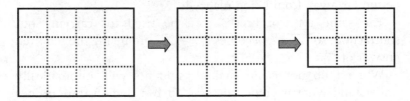

The resulting shape reveals $\frac{6}{12}$ or $\frac{1}{2}$ of the original size.

Reversing the order of the folds will obviously produce the same final outcome, and by doing this students can experience in a practical way the commutative property of multiplying fractions.

Clearly, this paper-folding approach of computing with fractions does not always reveal the lowest common denominator: for example, when working with pairs of fractions whose denominators are not co-prime, folding the paper into, say, quarters and sixths will produce twenty-fourths and not the required twelfths. However, if students have been getting to grips with these different computations, recognizing that certain amounts of twenty-fourths can be reduced to values with other denominators should not be too complex a step to take.

Because the process is robust, students can try adding, subtracting, dividing and multiplying different pairs of fractions with any two denominators. Clearly, the physicality of the situation means that when the size of the denominator becomes large, say greater than ten, the folding process becomes tedious. The ultimate aim is for students to shift from the practical paper-folding situation to producing a pencil and paper or a mental computation. Again, this shift from the concrete to the abstract will take on a different rate of realization for different students, and this is the basis of differentiated learning. Such decisions are navigated by students and negotiated by the classroom teacher, not by any textbook author.

As an extension, students can add pairs of fractions where both have a numerator of 1. The aim here is for students to see how the numbers connect together, thus leading to the generalization of $1/a + 1/b = \dfrac{a + b}{ab}$

A more complex challenge is for students to try to generalize what happen when fractions of the form $\frac{a}{b} + \frac{c}{d}$ are added together. I do not have any particular way of opening up this realization, other than allowing students to gather sufficient information and using this to seek a general result. What is important here is that students have a reason to carry out lots of calculations in order to seek the general result; this is different to students being given a procedure and applying it without understanding how the procedure works.

Student responsibility and making decisions

The strategy of asking students to do as many calculations as they feel necessary, to gain confidence and achieve competence, is an important principle for creating an environment where students take responsibility for their learning and make decisions for themselves. The teacher clearly cannot do the learning for them, so it is important to create a climate where students know what to do in order to become more skilled at something. When students are given the task of deciding how much they need to do to understand the mathematics involved, an important shift takes place: away from doing something because they have been told to do so, and towards doing something because they recognize the value of making progress.

One could argue that students could equally be given a textbook and encouraged to do as many of the questions in an exercise as they feel they need to. This is an interesting strategy and one I would not disagree with: however, this is more about the culture of the classroom than the intrinsic value of the resource – a key aspect of students taking responsibility is recognizing a need and having interest in what they are doing. Finding tasks that are intrinsically challenging and puzzling is one way of developing interest.

Writing about and writing-up mathematics

A further approach that can be applied in many mathematics lessons is students writing about what they have been doing and what they have understood. This process is intended to help them consolidate and deepen their understanding and to make explicit their implicit knowledge. Other reasons for students writing about mathematics is to help them recognize that 'writing' is not just something that happens in other subject areas. To encourage students to write as a way of becoming better at mathematics is to help break down barriers about what does and what does not constitute learning. This is important in mathematics if students are to perceive learning as a connected, joined-up experience.

Writing about mathematics also provides valuable contexts for students to practise literacy skills: ideally, students will likewise develop their mathematical skills in other subject areas (I develop this in Chapter 7).

Alternative spending plans for department capitation

Not buying textbooks means departmental money can be used for many other purposes such as buying equipment, software licences, paying for the printing of copies of a range of different grid papers and purchasing class sets of different types of calculators (simple, scientific, graphic). Every department can benefit from becoming institutional members of one or both professional associations for mathematics teaching, the Association of Teachers of Mathematics and the Mathematical Association. These associations produce marvellous journals and publications full of ideas for use in classrooms; any departmental meeting could easily begin with an article from a journal as a stimulus for discussion.

The type of resources a department has available and the different way these are used forms the pedagogical basis of a department and underpins the culture of what kind of things happen in mathematics lessons. If the central resource for a department is a textbook or a published scheme, and this guides teaching and learning in the department, this will have a significant impact upon departmental pedagogy.

At the beginning of this chapter I referred to the use of problem-solving approaches to teaching. I shall complete this chapter by looking at some problems that are incredibly 'simple' to pose yet provide students with much to think about and work on. They are all accessible, in terms of students needing only basic mathematical knowledge to proceed, yet can be explored at different depths. All of these ideas can be found in publications produced by the mathematics subject associations.

Diagonal through a rectangle

On 2cm-square grid paper, draw a rectangle. With a straight edge, carefully draw a diagonal. Count how many squares the diagonal passes through. In the example below the rectangle has dimensions of 6 by 3 and the diagonal passes through 6 squares.

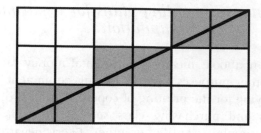

The problem is to see how the dimensions of any rectangle relate to the number of squares the diagonal passes through. If rectangles are chosen where the dimensions are co-prime, the solution looks obvious. However, once the dimensions share a common divisor (as in the example above), the earlier solution will need adapting. An extension task could be to work out how many unit cubes the 3D diagonal of a cuboid passes through when going from bottom front left corner to top back right corner.

More paper-folding, and some cutting

Take a rectangular piece of paper and fold it in half along its long edge. Now cut an isosceles right-angled triangle off one corner of the folded piece of paper. Which corner this triangle has been cut from will determine what the shape looks like when it is unfolded. What different solutions are there? What happens if the original piece of paper has been folded twice along (a) different edges and (b) the same edge? (c) What about three folds?

There are opportunities here for students to engage in some mind-imagery (see Chapter 5), to imagine and predict what will happen as different folds are made and different pieces are cut off.

Skewed Pascal

Instead of starting Pascal's Triangle arrangement with the numbers 1 and 1, what happens if we start with 1 and 2, i.e.

```
                  1    2
              1   3    2
          1   4   5    2
      1   5   9   7    2
  1   6   14  16  9    2
```

As can be observed, different number sequences emerge and, as with the 'ordinary' Pascal arrangement, these sequences run each way down the diagonals and are different order polynomials, constant, linear, quadratic, cubic and so on. While some students might generate patterns and look for connections, other could be encouraged to try to produce generalizations. In the above arrangement we have different linear and quadratic sequences depending upon whether we move diagonally from left to right or right to left. Generalizing the generalizations (starting with 1 and 3 then with 1 and 4 and so on) would be a further challenge. Any squares-on-a-chessboard spotter may recognize the emergence of the 1, 5, 14 ... sequence: in this context it is the beginning of a cubic sequence and has been generated by summing the square numbers.

	Sequences from top left to bottom right	Sequences from top right to bottom left
Linear	$n \to 2n - 1$	$n \to n + 1$
Quadratic	$n \to n^2$	$n \to \frac{n}{2}(n + 3)$

Another challenge is to see what happens as sequences are taken backwards:

7, 5, 3, 1, ⁻1, ⁻3, ... or 14, 9, 5, 2, 0, ⁻1, ⁻1, 0, 2, ...

From the starting point, therefore, there can be a number of possible developments, yet the idea is so easy to set up in the first instance. With a younger class, I would want them to have met Pascal's triangle before (see Chapter 14), and this is an issue of long-term planning.

Getting the Buggers to Add Up

Seeing what mathematical content emerges through such problems and thinking about how to present such ideas as problem-solving challenges will help develop students' skills in *using* and *applying* mathematics.

202

14

MATHEMATICS
AND ...

In this chapter I fly a few kites and look at the possibility of broadening the scope of mathematics teaching in terms of parents (including guardians and carers), primary school liaison and mathematics within a mathematics department. I begin by looking at the feasibility of working with the parents of the students we teach. There is a strong case for prioritizing time to work with adults, to share perspectives and to help them make sense of the changes that continually take place.

There are many positive benefits of opening classroom doors to show parents what happens and why it happens; this is all part of a process of transparency. My experience reveals that seeking to rationalize why I teach mathematics the way I do in order to communicate and justify this rationale to parents is an excellent way of causing me to check out the approaches I use and strengthen my pedagogy. There are more important reasons for working with parents: to build confidence in how their children are being taught mathematics and to help some of them understand why 'it was never like this when I was at school!'.

Mathematics and parents/guardians

Welcoming adults into mathematics classrooms so they can experience what their children typically do in school is central to organizing 'Mathematics for Parents' evenings; I have always found these to be extraordinarily positive events. Communicating the way a department teaches mathematics to adults is an important aspect of developing home–school relationships; fostering these can have particularly valuable outcomes. Some of the best consultation evenings I have been involved in have been when the mathematics department organized such evenings, usually in collaboration with the school Parent Teacher Association. Every one of these events proved enjoyable, informative and, because of the different formats used, was always interesting and valuable.

Adults come to such events with a range of expectations about how their children should or ought to be taught mathematics, and with questions about how much help adults are able to provide or should try to give their children. Some, for example, might want to discuss how they might best help their children when they 'cannot do their homework'. Adults also have varying degrees of confidence in their own mathematical capability; some will relive the anxieties they felt when they were at school, others will be more confident and may use mathematics as a regular part of the work they do. The issue of seeking to cater for adults with such a wide range of experience, confidence and expectations about how mathematics *should* be taught runs parallel to working with a class of adolescents.

To try to cater for such a range I use different formats:

- whole-group introduction;
- offering 'potted' versions of sequences of lessons;
- workshops of collections of ideas;
- whole-group plenary.

Whole-group introduction

With this format I use a 'lecture' style approach, and because any lecture I give involves active participation by the audience, I use this strategy with parents. One such 'lecture' is to offer parents a task which helps them see how mathematics can be easy to make a start on and reveals an important difference between the arithmetic of counting and the mathematics of pattern-spotting, predicting, conjecturing and generalizing. The following task is one way of illustrating this.

1. On a piece of 1cm-squared paper, draw a 7-by-7cm square.
2. Start from the top lefthand square count *one, two and three* and colour in the fourth.
3. Now count again from the next (fifth) square, *one, two and three* and shade in the next square. (When the end of the first row is reached, start again from the left-hand side of the next row.)
4. Continue shading in every fourth square.

At some point during the counting and shading the pattern below emerges and can be described as [Grid 7, +4]

1	*2*	*3*	**4**	*1*	*2*	*3*
4	*1*	*2*				

This is a set of diagonal lines, and once recognized it is likely that shading in by counting will be abandoned and shading according to the pattern will take over. At this point the counting stops and mathematics takes over. Some developments are:

- Find the shading pattern for different rules using the same grid width.
- Change the width of the original grid to, say, size 8 and then see what happens when the +4 rule is applied.
- Look for connections between add rules and grid widths.
- Classify common types of patterns that occur.

We could also introduce the notation of vectors to describe the patterns between diagonal lines of shaded squares. This simple, accessible problem is an excellent demonstration of what is meant by 'doing mathematics'.

A key feature is getting parents to do some mathematics and, from this experience, to discuss issues about how their children engage with mathematics. In a curriculum based upon problem-solving, it is incredibly easy to offer parents any number of problems to work on; however, I can imagine the reaction if I were to give them a textbook and invite them to 'Work through exercise A on page 27'!

'Potted' versions of sequences of lessons

The idea behind this format is to offer some starting points for a lesson that leads to developing mathematical thinking over a sequence of lessons. There are umpteen ideas that might be used, and I offer three.

Routes on a grid

This idea is about finding all possible routes on a square-dot grid from the top left-hand corner point **S** to every other point on the grid. Normally as a starting point (say with a Year 7 class), there could be some discussion about how many different routes there are if there were no rules. At some point, by introducing or discussing the need to reduce the number of ways of moving to **R**ight and **D**own, a more systematic collection of routes can be found leading to the following result.

S●	**1**●	**1**●	**1**●
1●	**2**●	**3**●	**4**●
1●	**3**●	**6**●	**10**●
1●	**4**●	**10**●	**20**●

These are, of course, numbers from Pascal's Triangle arrangement (although this array of numbers was known in India and China long before Pascal), and the diagram needs to be turned through 45° to view the arrangement in its usual format. Given the enormous importance of Pascal's Triangle and the number of places it arises in various guises in mathematics, the importance of introducing this idea early in children's mathematical experience cannot be understated. As such, this is a valuable way of helping adults see that mathematics is a collection of connected ideas.

Predicting values on a 5-by-5 and a 6-by-6 grid opens up one way of looking for and developing the arrangement. Once the values are established there are many number patterns that can be found and explored. This opens up opportunities to demonstrate how a seemingly simple, accessible starting point can be developed, thus catering for the different mathematical aspirations of children (see 'Skewed Pascal' in Chapter 12).

Four in a line

This is a simple game played by two people, each with a different colour of pegs and a pegboard. The idea of the game is for players to place pegs on the board in turn, and the winner is the person who makes an uninterrupted line of 4 pegs of their colour. Lines can be made at any angle, so we are not restricted to horizontal, vertical or 45° diagonals.

Once a winning line has been made it can be recorded as a coordinate pair (so an origin will need to be defined). Predicting points at either end of each line, exploring the mid-point of each line segment or trying to write the equation of each line will provide further challenges. This task can demonstrate the value of using practical equipment. Also, by collecting a number of winning lines together on the board, we can see how the task can lead to work on coordinates, negative numbers and equations of lines, as well as developing some of the important strategic skills inherent in the game. Furthermore, because the information has been created by students (or in this instance by adults), issues of 'ownership' of the information and problem-solving can be raised.

Some speedy data-handling

This task is so beautifully simple, yet engages everyone in using and applying a range of data-handling skills. On an overhead transparency either make a photocopy of page 9 of the ATM publication *Learning and teaching mathematics without a textbook* (Ollerton, 2002), or draw between 60 and 70 star shapes and project these onto a screen/board for approximately ten seconds. Then switch off the projector. I ask everyone individually to write an estimate of how many stars they think they saw, collect the answers in and write each estimate on the board. This takes no more than a couple of minutes. With all the data on the board I ask them to think about different ways we might use it, to agree upon a value that is representative of the information on the board. This question promotes discussion about how the information might be used, inevitably culminating in different types of averages: the mean, the median and the mode.

Year 7 students often suggest finding the value half way between the largest and the smallest estimate. Using the information to consider what sense any of these averages make is a key part of this task and, as previously mentioned, there is a beautiful simplicity in setting up a task which holds so much opportunity for developing in-depth thinking. Further calculations are possible, such as drawing histograms, using a sample 'window' to count a fraction of the whole number or asking the group to make a second estimate. This usually produces a decrease in the size of the range as more people make a second estimate that is closer to the actual answer.

A workshop of ideas

When using a workshop-style format, adults are invited to spend approximately one hour working on typical problems. This involves writing problems on separate pieces of card, with the equipment or grid paper likely to be needed arranged next to each one. The visual impact of walking into a classroom with lots of equipment, coloured papers and different grid papers creates an excellent flavour of what working in a mathematics classroom feels like. Below are typical examples. Having a range of problems, puzzles and games of varying complexity means everyone can find something to work on. In this more relaxed atmosphere, adults can have informal discussions about the nature of the work and how the ideas are intended to help their children develop mathematical skills and become active problem solvers.

Make all the different solid cuboids from 24 linking cubes. For each calculate its surface area. What do you notice?

Write the multiples of 9 until you see a pattern. Make a note of other patterns you find in the multiples of 9.

Find a way of working out the average shoe size of everyone in the room. Draw a picture to illustrate your work.	Draw a graph of the multiples of 2. What does a graph of one more than the multiples of 2 look like?
Make all the different shapes by joining 5 squares together edge to full edge. Describe the symmetry of each shape.	Think of a number, add 5, double the result, take away 9 then subtract the number you first thought of. What happens? Why?
Place each of the numbers 1, 2, 3, 4, 5, 6, 7, 8 and 9 in a 3 by 3 square so that each line of three numbers adds up to the same total.	If 16 is always the 'answer' make up some questions. Use different numbers and types of operations.

Plenary

Bringing everyone together to share perceptions is a key part of such an event. If ideas have been worked on in different classrooms, one part of the plenary could be to group parents together and ask them to discuss what they have been doing and learning. This approach is a way of modelling how parents might similarly discuss with their children what they have been doing at school. Those parents for whom mathematics may be a mystery usually value discussion about how they can help their children, particularly those who lack confidence in their mathematical capabilities. A useful strategy is for parents to ask probing questions, to gently encourage their children to explain what they are doing and, where applicable, what they are stuck on. Quite often such questioning can be the catalyst for a child to make sense of what they are stuck on, purely as a consequence of trying to verbalize it. Of course, such approaches to questioning are skills that teachers build up over a lifetime, and we cannot expect parents to become expert questioners overnight; the important issue is opening up the possibility, and the importance, of asking questions. Again, this is a key part of home and school being supportive frameworks for children's development.

An interesting aspect of such events is how frequently parents are often more concerned with trying to reach a solution to a problem they have worked on earlier in the evening. It is almost as though the challenge of figuring something out takes on a greater importance; I am not particularly surprised by this kind of response, as it fits closely with my understanding of the use of puzzlement as a strong motivator for learning. When parents become hooked by mathematics and by the natural desire to reach a solution to a puzzle, this is something worth celebrating. At one evening parents became so deeply engaged in the mathematics that at the end, as they were leaving, I had to remind them we had not yet discussed the 'main' issues relating to the latest government pronouncement on the teaching of mathematics. Given the mathematical buzz in the room, this did not seem important. Under such circumstances I was confident of gaining parental support for the way I taught mathematics in the future.

Whatever ideas are chosen, the important issue is to try to recreate for parents what being in a mathematics classroom feels like. As suggested earlier, this might for some be about reliving painful experiences. Others will have an opportunity to reconceptualize what learning mathematics entails. The more information parents have about how their children are encouraged to learn mathematics, the greater the possibility of sharing perspectives, encouraging openness, gaining valuable support and finding common ground. Nurturing parents' confidence that the teaching methods are sound, carefully considered and appropriately applied to their children's mathematical development is of paramount importance.

Mathematics and cross-phase liaison

What kind of information do secondary school teachers want or need about the children they are going to teach for the first time?

What quantity of information will a teacher have time to read, take cognisance of and use to plan lessons? What kind of information can a secondary school teacher realistically make use of? Questions such as these might be a focus for a primary teacher to consider with regard to the information they provide and how it will benefit children and secondary school teachers. Just how much time primary teachers put into the records they write and to what extent such information is used by secondary school colleagues is something worth considering ... perhaps before such records are compiled in the future.

Of much greater importance than the quantity of information is sharing the ways children are taught and how children experience learning in different phases. Having spent my first two years teaching in a primary school, I always find it refreshing to visit primary classrooms. I always gain a vibrant sense of interesting environments, where walls are plastered with wonderful, colourful displays and classrooms are stimulating places.

On one occasion, in 1998, I was invited to do some cross-phase mathematics liaison with a local primary school and was acutely reminded of the responsibility and autonomy young children are encouraged to develop. This was exemplified during a lesson on scale drawing. I set up a situation where pairs of children drew an outline of each other on the back of old sheets of wallpaper and used this outline to take measurements of height, arm length, leg length, shoulder width, and so on. The main aim was to make quarter size scale models of themselves: the mathematics was measuring and quartering (halving and halving again).

The class worked on this task and after a few minutes one girl asked me if she could put all her information onto a spreadsheet. At this point I looked around for the class teacher to see what the procedure was for using the computer. The girl, however, stopped me in my tracks when she glibly said she knew how to use a spreadsheet and people in her class used the computer whenever they needed to! Gobsmacked, I marvelled at her sense of independence ... her teacher had clearly encouraged such behaviour and expected the children to work in this way.

I learnt how young children were encouraged to develop and the kind of expectations placed upon them. Having such insights can only have a positive benefit upon my teaching, particularly in terms of recognizing the kind of learning environments primary-aged children are used to and the degree of responsibility they are encouraged to take. Of course, the nature of secondary phase education means students are taught in separate subject areas for most of their time. This has a significant impact because children move from teacher to teacher, each with their different expectations. However, some secondary schools make use of more integrated approaches, combining certain subjects together for the first year of secondary school. Other schools seek to minimize the number of staff who teach the new intake, thus creating a situation where fewer teachers have a greater knowledge of the students.

With regard to mathematics, creating learning environments where more active, discursive, problem-solving type approaches are used, and where greater emphasis is put upon the creation of display work, student presentations and students producing their own 'topic' booklets will help, in part, to bridge the primary–secondary transfer.

Mathematics and mathematics teachers

Sometimes I prioritize my time to do some mathematics, although this does not happen as often as I would like; this is hardly surprising given the busy and multi-faceted nature of the job of teaching. However, when I actually engage in some mathematics I revisit my own enjoyment of the discipline and this reminds me why I teach mathematics. I strengthen my rationale for teaching and this inevitably means I can take refreshed enthusiasms with me into my classrooms.

Involvement in a Professional Association

Creating opportunities to work on mathematics and share this experience with others might be considered an unaffordable

213

luxury, a rarity. One of the more important influences on my mathematical and pedagogical development is being an active member of the Association of Teachers of Mathematics (ATM). I have learnt a great deal by working with other members, through curriculum working groups, regional conferences and branch meetings. There is also the annual Easter Conference, when I devote four days to working on mathematics and catching up with other members of the association. I engage in the pleasures of problem-solving and the thrill of exercising atrophied and rusty parts of my brain.

Such an occurrence happened at the 2003 ATM conference, during a session organized by Lyndon Baker and Ian Harris. The group was presented with the following problem:

$$(115)^2 = 11 \times 12[25]$$

The '25' in the square brackets in the calculation emerges from 5^2, and this forms the tens and the units digits when combined with the product formed by calculating 11×12. Thus the complete answer becomes 13,225.

We were asked to see if this always worked; this led me to question why it worked. The problem can be developed to see what happens when we square numbers ending in a 6, a 7 or any digit. I worked on this with another person called Sam. As we began to make sense of what happened and why the result occurred, we became more and more engaged. We developed the task to prove why it worked and what mathematical adjustments would be needed if the unit digit were something other than a 5. However, in order to solve the problem, to reach an end point, we chose not to work on any of the other problems that Ian and Lyndon kept offering to the group. There are issues here which I develop below.

Time to reflect

Finding time to reflect upon certain issues is not always easy. All too often, as teachers, we have to move on to the next task without having time to take breath; reflecting upon what we have been doing to determine what the implications might be for future action can be highly problematic. Yet it is only when I reflect upon something that I open up the possibility of making changes to my thinking and, therefore, adapt my practice.

One outcome of attending the Baker/Harris session was to consider a particular issue that caught my attention. This was the issue of pace. In the session, I needed time to work on the $(115)^2$ problem at a pace I felt comfortable. This initially involved some negotiation with another person and an agreement to keep working on the problem and develop it in some depth rather than moving on to another problem. We certainly did not want anyone else to tell us the solution they had devised. The teacher, in this instance, respected our decision to continue with the problem rather than working on other problems he had prepared.

The experience of being a learner helped confirm for me the importance of having choice (particularly about the pace I worked at), of being able to negotiate what I worked on and, most importantly, not being hurried along to finish something at the teacher's pace. My pace of learning was more important than the plans my teacher had formulated.

If 'pace', therefore, in a mathematics classroom, is construed as a whole class 'moving on' to the next idea and is about 'the' speed at which this is intended to happen, then I have many concerns about the effect of pace upon students' development. Learners need time to work on ideas, to tackle problems in different depths; they need time to think about and sort out ideas for themselves. If pace is defined as the speed of the class at the expense of individuals having time to work on a problem, such a notion might serve to act as an unhelpful and anti-educational construct.

Some days later I discussed the same mathematical problem with Nick Eyres, a nonagenarian friend and retired mathematics teacher (and, sadly, recently deceased). Nick's ideas appear in the ATM publication *Forty Problems for the Classroom*. His response was: 'Well, its obvious . . . and what's more, we can use the same process to calculate $(3.5)^2$.' What I found so interesting in his response was the fact that although this problem was 'new' to me it was something he knew about, had used in his teaching and which had been 'around' for decades ... I had just not come across it before. This begs the question about what other problems have been lost in the mists of time, and how problems used decades ago would be highly appropriate for today's and tomorrow's mathematics classrooms.

There are several further important issues here. The first is that, because I opened myself up to working on some mathematics, I met an idea new to myself. Second, by working with another person, we developed it, symbolized it and eventually proved why it worked. The third is that by being in the position of learner, I engaged in pedagogical thoughts about the impact of certain ideas (pace) upon classroom organization. Fourth, I had the satisfaction of solving a problem. Finally, I widened my range of ideas for use in the classroom. Add to this a pinch of the Baker/Harris zany approach and I possibly have an opportunity to enhance my teaching style as well.

Doing some mathematics at department meetings

As a young teacher, I remember my head of department starting a meeting by casting a whole lot of ATM MATs (see Chapter 5) onto the table and inviting colleagues to discuss what mathematics they might be able to get out of them. For the first 15 or so minutes we 'played' with the equipment and discussed the potential for using them in our teaching. On other occasions we considered what use we could make of other types of equipment. Discussing mathematics for the first part of a meeting and/or developing curriculum ideas for modules within the departmental scheme of work was something we did on a semi-regular basis. This produced a collaborative and evolutionary approach to curriculum development, and all members of the department had some responsibility for, and ownership of, what and how we taught. Having such opportunities to discuss mathematics at the beginning of a meeting was a marvellous way of sharing different teaching approaches. This also meant that business agenda items were appropriately relegated to matters of secondary importance.

Seeking a balance between curriculum development opportunities and the need to get through the business agenda is a critical issue for heads of department to consider. One aspect of this is to decide how much departmental business can be conducted outside department meetings.

Prioritizing time to work on some mathematics can however be difficult, particularly when there are so many new initiatives showering down upon schools from central government and local authorities. Tests to be taught to and targets to be 'met' can, if we let them, have a substantial and damaging effect upon how mathematics is taught and learnt. Whenever prescription from 'above' starts to run counter to a department's thoughtfully considered and soundly constructed pedagogy, we need to utilize skills and find the strength to resist unhelpful pressures. I firmly believe in honest and open argument, and if this fails moving towards a state of healthy disrespect and, if absolutely necessary, gentle subversion. The greater the resolve we have about the ways we want to teach mathematics, the stronger our pedagogy about how mathematics is most effectively learnt, and the ways we try to build effective learning environments is all part of professional development. This is something departments can do first and foremost in-house. Using departmental meetings to exchange individual enthusiasms, share expertise and excitement for the subject, and discuss lesson ideas that 'worked' is fundamental to professional development. This can be achieved by doing mathematics.

Mathematics and assessment

There has been a massive amount of important research and writing into assessment, such as the work of Cooper and Dunne, Morgan and Watson, Black and Wiliam and the Assessment Reform Group. I do not intend to write a review of this literature or an essay on types of assessment: formative, summative, diagnostic, etc. I do intend to offer some real experiences of approaches to assessment I have found valuable. Before doing this, however, I consider the following 'what' and 'how' type questions:

1.   What do I think is important about assessment?
2.   How can I integrate assessment into my classroom practice?

To answer the first question I must consider what I actually do with any information I might collect about a student. I must recognize the frailty of any assumptions I make based upon the information I receive. If I am to decide upon the kind of question I might ask a student so I can diagnose what they understand in order to provide a) a clearer explanation; b) some practice questions; or c) some deepening, extension tasks, I must inevitably try to 'connect' with the student's present cognition. To achieve this I must be making all kinds of instantaneous assessments and, as such, I am inevitably engaging with the second question. What I consider important about assessment, therefore, cannot be detached from how I carry out assessments. Although there is a great deal of pressure on schools to report students 'levels' of achievement (matched against national criteria), I question the notion of what a level means and the spurious, pseudo-objectification of assigning levels to student achievement. The most important and positive form of assessment is the one that takes place moment-by-moment and day-by-day in lessons. The second most important form is that which enables students to reveal both their understandings and their misconceptions relating to the mathematics they have been doing, and I develop this below.

On pages 239–40 I mention the idea of students writing the test questions themselves. Briefly, the approach works as follows:

- we review the work a class has done over the past term;
- we discuss what kind of test questions would 'fairly' assess their understanding;
- students write questions;
- I collate and decide upon which questions to use and add others;
- the chosen questions are typed up and the completed test paper is given to students.

Two important reasons for using this approach are ceding responsibility and ownership of assessment processes to students.

A third reason is my belief that when students write questions about what they have been learning this simultaneously enhances understanding, and I develop this issue in the next chapter.

Another approach to assessment is for students to build up a folder or a portfolio of their achievement. To do this, students need opportunities to work on modules or extended pieces of mathematics, and to be encouraged to write about the work they have done. Completed modules of work can be stored in folders, which students can use to self-assess their achievement and which teachers can use to make professional, summative judgements on achievement. One of the interesting aspects of a GCSE course which was jointly created by the Association of Teachers of Mathematics and the Southern Examining Group was students producing folders of work. These folders became a record of students' mathematical achievements, and at moderation meetings were used to standardize GCSE grades. Three important outcomes were as follows:

1. As teachers examined the work in students' folders, we were able to determine and agree upon GCSE grades – and this did not in general prove to be a lengthy process.
2. We decided to utilize the exact same approach (of students creating folders of work) at Key Stage 3. The impact of this was to develop extended modules of work on a coursework-type model throughout the 11–16 age range.
3. An unintended outcome was the massive amount of sharing and professional development that occurred. This was because we not only discussed the work students had produced, we also found out about the ideas and resources teachers had used in order for students to produce the work.

As such, an exercise intended as a moderation process became a strong professional development forum. Ideas and information about resources were shared, teaching approaches were disseminated and everyone benefited. Methodologies were translated into the rest of the age range, and summative assessment was not solely based upon the scores from internal tests.

For me to be confident that I am professionally capable, along with students, to engage in valuable modes of assessment, the schemes of work I help create must implicitly question the value of test scores and explicitly provide opportunities for students to demonstrate their depth of mathematical understanding.

15

DARING TO BE DIFFERENT

In this chapter I consider some accepted orthodoxys regarding teaching and learning mathematics in schools, and explore the possibilities of working differently.

Teachers undertake a vast number of tasks. These include lesson-planning, preparing resources, assessing students' work and dealing with youngsters – some of whom may have behavioural difficulties, or problems at home. We meet parents, run extra-curricular activities, attend departmental meetings, pastoral meetings and whole-school meetings. We respond to a plethora of government curriculum and funding initiatives; some of these are short-term and frequently changing. Each of these tasks, and others not listed, require varying amounts of energy and need to be dealt with on different levels of complexity. Is it any wonder that some cannot be given the amount of time we might wish, in order to achieve a desired quality of outcome? Time is absolute, we cannot stretch it out or squeeze more things in; we can only prioritize what we choose to spend our time on within the limitations of what is possible ... even for miracle workers.

My experience, however, of working in dozens of schools and with hundreds of teachers, suggests mathematics is largely taught through exercises based upon published schemes. Investigative work tends to be separated from mainstream mathematics lessons and is frequently taught in a bolt-on fashion. Such practice may be driven by schemes of work, a head of department, school policies, or in response to inspection. In this chapter I discuss some alternative ways of working, not to suggest change for change's sake, but to consider how some changes can 'create time' by meaning less time is spent on certain other tasks. I look in particular at marking habits, consider implications for setting homework, and return to the issue of marking by looking at types of activities within lessons that avoid the need for teachers to do 'traditional' forms of marking.

Marking books, marking time, 'traditional' marking is a bit of a bind

One of the more boring aspects of being a mathematics teacher must surely be that of taking home armfuls of students' exercise books for marking. In my experience this figures as one of the biggest yawns imaginable ... by comparison, washing up seems an exciting and creative activity. Spending time putting ticks and kisses against students' answers and possibly adding a brief comment never convinced me of the value of what I was doing. I often felt it would have been far more valuable if I had been able to say something to each student, particularly when it appeared some had made a simple error and others had seemingly lost the plot altogether ... perhaps it was more a case of them losing my plot! Worse still were feelings that I must have been speaking in another language; given that mathematics does have its own language, perhaps I was. Even worse was a deep-down feeling that students would pay little if any attention to my efforts marking their books; this added to the sense of the meaninglessness of the turgid task and the time I spent in my state of futility.

It is useful, therefore, to consider what kind of marking is worth doing in order to decide what value and what impact different forms of marking have upon students' development. This issue came strongly into focus during a school in-service day several years ago, when all staff looked at a small sample of students' exercise books from different subject areas. The intention was to gain a wider perspective on the kind of feedback colleagues offered and what the individual student's wider experience of feedback looked like.

My attention was taken by comments written by different teachers to one student, who found academic work a considerable struggle. To my shock I found very few supportive or positive comments. Such was my concern at what I read I noted down some of the comments (I have not included comments such as 'date' and 'heading').

Incomplete	*Very untidy, poor homework*
More observations should have been made	*Untidy ★&!?+★!★$ (second word illegible)*
Late — no work	*Writing untidy*
I cannot read some of this work	*Bien*
You've missed the point	*Spellings*
Spellings	
	Good so far
There are so many bad spellings	*Your spelling is awful*
Better here, slightly	*Very poor spellings*
You silly person	
Good idea, poor spelling	*Untidy*
You've absolutely wasted your time then	*Messy spellings*

The outcome for me was quite profound and deeply disturbing. Gaining a wider picture of the kind of comments being written had a direct impact upon my practice. This was to avoid writing such comments in the future and become more acutely aware of how such comments might appear to students. Just what effect such comments might have upon the student was worth considering and I formulated some questions:

- Did this student know she was not very good at spelling?
- What would you think of this collection of comments if you were the girl's parent?
- What value do such comments have in supporting learning?
- Was writing such comments an effective use of teachers' time?
- Is this experience similar for teachers in other schools?

Some of these questions are clearly rhetorical; I would be very surprised if the student did not know she had severe difficulties with spelling. A more important issue is how she might be supported to become better at spelling. This would require time and support: however, if a teacher's valuable time is taken up with writing such comments, this could be construed as not only a waste of time but also a lost opportunity to create a more encouraging climate for the student to develop her talents. If a similar occurrence happens in other schools and if little advantage is gained by students or by teachers, it is worth considering who benefits from this kind of marking.

Do we carry out brief tick/kiss marking so parents and guardians perceive us to be carrying out our jobs properly? Are we doing it because students' books are checked by the head of department or by other senior colleagues? Is it because school policy dictates that subject teachers set and mark homework on a regular basis? Are such policies produced for inspection purposes? Are students conditioned to expect this to happen? What kind of marking and feedback promotes achievement?

There are issues here of busy teachers marking and providing feedback while being under a great deal of pressure to demonstrate they are doing their jobs 'properly'. However, one of the most important aspects of teaching lies in lesson-planning, and the more interesting ideas we can come up with, the more interested our students are likely to be.

Planning lessons must also take account of the way we expect students to work, both inside and outside the classroom, and the different ways we want students to respond to show what they have learnt. Some outcomes could be for students to produce a poster, do a write-up or give a presentation. When a sequence of lessons is planned with the intention of developing in-depth understanding, and where different students are expected to achieve different end-points, this inevitably has an impact upon the type of homework students might be encouraged to do ... I feel a confession coming on.

Confession time

As a form tutor, I was often aware of some students copying each other's homework answers. This would probably be to meet a deadline of handing in their exercise books during registration time. I confess I never prevented such behaviour, mainly because I was more concerned about the futility of taking such actions and whether or not it was my role to police when or where my form group did their homework. I was equally conscious that I did not wish my relationship with my tutees to be undermined or affected by demands made upon them by colleagues' methods of organization. This may indicate I was unsupportive of colleagues' efforts ... but a confession is, after all, about being honest!

Those students who had not completed their homework the previous evening (or that morning on the school bus) were clearly only wanting to 'play the game' and avoid some kind of sanction. All too often I felt I had to set homework, not to enhance students' learning, but because this was the school policy or because a parent had complained to the headteacher about their child not having any homework for a period of time. However, what if a school policy actually gets in the way of effective learning? What if a policy leads teachers to setting off-the-cuff, unplanned tasks that are more for the sake of fulfilling the policy than for the benefit of students? What if a policy is no more than window-dressing for senior management, for parents or (perish the thought) for the impending arrival of Ofsted?

My concern is that homework can take on a disproportionate dimension and can be a root cause of conflict between teachers and students, adolescents and parents 'culminating in the cry from the kitchen: 'Have you done your homework yet ... You're not going out until ...' (a door is heard closing with a loud bang).

Homework, homogeneity and heuristics

Whether homework is intended to extend or develop some work students are doing in school, whether it is used for practice, consolidation or revision purposes or whether it is used to collect information for use in a future lesson, the central issue is about planning. Thinking about the kind of homework task that complements classwork clearly requires careful planning: however, this can be difficult, as we cannot predict what different students will achieve in a lesson. Of course, we have moments in lessons when setting an unplanned homework task suddenly seems far more appropriate than the one we may have planned, just as sometimes we come up with the inspirational idea as we walk down the corridor to a lesson.

In any class there is going to be wide variations in students' home backgrounds, the support systems they have at home and the love and encouragement they are given. As such, any work we ask students to do outside school needs to acknowledge that such differences exist, and requires care and sensitivity both in terms of tasks posed and our expectations of what anyone might achieve. Some schools now offer homework clubs either at lunchtime or after school, and I feel such initiatives potentially offer positive ways for supporting students in doing homework.

Examples of homework tasks likely to gain different responses are:

1. Find out about the Fibonacci sequence.
2. Count how many electrical appliances there are at home.
3. Find out how good your Mum, Dad or guardian are at long multiplication, long division or even at solving algebraic equations.
4. Keep a record of how much television you watch over a week.
5. Keep a record of who does the household chores during a typical week.
6. Explain to someone at home something you have learnt in mathematics today.
7. Draw a map of your journey from school to home.
8. Find out about different counting systems.
9. Make a poster, on a piece of A4 paper, to describe something you have understood about the work we had been doing in today's lesson.

Example 3) frequently causes some amusement as well as creating the conditions for some home–school dialogue. In response to 8), as well as receiving counting systems from different historical periods and in different languages, somebody once came back with the 'yan, tan, tethera ...': a system for counting sheep. The poster resulting from 9 can form an 'instant' display (I develop this later in the chapter).

227

There are, of course, a vast number of problems and puzzles that students can be given to work on:

- Find all the consecutive sums of numbers from 1 up to whenever you get tired.
- Find all the possible ways of partitioning the numbers 3, 4, 5 and so on by addition.
- Find all the different answers that you can make using the digits 3, 7 and 8, in any order, with the operations + and × and brackets where appropriate.
- Find all the different ways of arranging six dots on 1cm grid paper so that no dot is more than 1cm away from another dot.
- Explain why the sum of three consecutive numbers is divisible by 3 but the sum of four consecutive numbers is not divisible by 4.

Each of these could be developed in a subsequent lesson, so that instead of homework being a continuation of something from a lesson, it becomes preparation work for a future lesson.

Homework can be used as an ongoing writing-up process. There are important issues here about student responsibility. Such homework tasks matched the way I organized student learning and were commensurate with the underlying principles behind schemes of work. Consequently I did not collect books in week after week. Instead, I adopted a very different style of marking and feedback, which I describe below.

Writing comments in response to students' work

To decide what kind of marking helps students become better mathematicians and better learners, it is useful to consider how any form of marking is likely to have a positive impact upon learning. One approach I found purposeful was to write comments of 50 to 150 words in length. This might sound a time-consuming task. However, because I only collected students' work in once every three or four weeks, this meant I redirected my marking time to writing formative comments and providing overall feedback. On some occasions this would be quite detailed, as illustrated in the second comment below. Collecting in students' work every three of four weeks did not mean I only ever saw each student's work every three or four weeks. During lessons I regularly made short written comments, perhaps suggesting something a student might try next. In this way I kept myself informed of students' ongoing progress while setting realistic agreed targets during lessons.

Below is a typical comment. Jane was a Year 10 student who had made considerable progress. In order to cajole her our relationship was one of mutual joking: I certainly got as good as I gave.

> There is some good work here Jane and further evidence that you are developing sound work habits that will help you achieve your potential in this subject. There are a couple of small errors that you could apply a brain cell or two to, however this apart you have achieved a good understanding of the ideas involved in transformations and matrices. You have again written a useful set of final thoughts and these are a further indication of the ideas you have understood. They also help me determine what kind of tasks I might need to offer you in the future to help you develop your mathematical thinking. I hope you told your Mum what a great cardigan I thought she knitted for you!

This next comment is a response to some work a Year 11 student did on trigonometry. On this occasion the module had lasted for five weeks, and while trigonometry was the central concept, students worked on a whole range of interconnected skills, from rounding up to a number of decimal places, to drawing graphs of sine functions. Kelly was a hardworking student who put a great deal of time into her work outside lessons.

> Another super piece of work Kelly again showing the depth of thought that you have taken your ideas to. Every aspect of your final write-up shows a careful approach. Your analysis of sine functions is really good and this level of mathematics takes the assessment of your work off the scale (at the higher end!) You

have set up and solved your own problems in order to work out lengths and angles in right-angled triangles. The further work using a clinometer clearly caused you some problems that you were able to engage with after some thought. Your final section really says it all. I find what you have written here very interesting indeed because you have clearly set out what you have gained and understood from this trigonometry project. I like the way you have described the need to use a calculator for carrying out a calculation as opposed to speeding up a calculation. So this is another excellent piece of work and looking to the future it will obviously be important that you can recognize when and how to use these skills in examinations. Now then, what can I nag you about?

Because I put this kind of concerted energy into providing feedback I made a point, when returning work, of asking students to read carefully what I had written; sometimes I asked them to write a comment in response. On other occasions I would ask them to show my comments to someone at home and request they ask this person to write a comment back to me. This was a further element to foster communication between home and school. If an opportunity arose to engage with students in an amusing way, perhaps by mentioning something related to a recent event, I might choose to add something of this nature to my comment. Thus, my mentioning Jane's cardigan in the first comment arose from the fact I had recently met her mother at a consultation evening.

Furthermore, as a consequence of word-processing my comments I had a record of what I had written and was able to store and recall comments when necessary. At consultation evenings, for instance, I would have my Amstrad (bright green screen and all) on the desk and be able to access all the comments I had written for each student I taught. This meant parents could read my comments if they wished. A further use for such comments was as an aide-mémoire when writing summative reports.

This type of feedback developed as a direct consequence of the coursework students did in Year 10 and Year 11, which eventually filtered down into Years 9, 8 and 7. Students usually wrote up three or four extended pieces of work each term (and this had a direct bearing upon the nature of the planning outlined in Chapter 10).

If we are to be able to prioritize time for planning we 'obviously' need to consider where this time is going to come from. As already mentioned, we cannot manufacture time, so it is important to cut down on the amount of time we spend on other aspects of the job. One such aspect is the amount and type of marking carried out. Below I offer some suggestions about the kinds of tasks that won't require us to take home armfuls of exercise books.

Tasks that won't require so much marking

The suggestions I offer not only cut back on traditional approaches to marking but also provide a richer, more varied diet of work modes for students. This in turn taps into different students' learning preferences; and so we become more effective teachers. This is, therefore, a double bonus, exchanging time given to boring types of marking for planning more interesting lessons.

Students producing posters

Posters can help enhance the classroom environment, as well as providing students with opportunities to demonstrate what they know; posters can be created out of just about any work students do and, as such, it is not necessary for posters to be 'pristine' or time-consuming. Indeed, putting up displays about ongoing ideas to stimulate discussion is just as valuable as posters produced when a topic is completed. A homework task I once gave to a Year 8 class was to make a poster on brightly coloured A4 paper to show something they had understood about the work we had been doing on factors, thus providing a summary of the main ideas the class had worked on.

Display can be used as a focus for discussion, to help develop students' understanding of a concept. For example, if I want to

231

focus attention on what happens when squares are drawn on the sides of triangles, I could set up the following task.

Give different pairs of students some pre-drawn triangles on squared grid paper, ensuring that some students only have triangles with an obtuse angle, some have right-angled triangles, and others have triangles whose angles are all acute. The task now is for students to draw squares on each side of their allocated triangles and calculate the area of each square. As diagrams are completed they can be quickly stuck on a wall, whereupon the class can be drawn together around the display to discuss what they notice about the information gathered. Whether I use such a task as a starting point for Pythagoras' theorem or whether I introduce this task once Pythagoras' relationship has already been established is a decision I make as part of my short-term ongoing lesson planning.

The same strategy can be used with other concepts. For example, some work on trigonometric functions might proceed as follows. Each student (or pair of students) is given a sheet of graph paper with $y = \text{Sin}x$ already drawn on it. They are then asked to draw just one of the following graphs, super-imposing it on the graph paper supplied:

$$y = 2\text{Sin}x,\ y = \tfrac{1}{2}\,\text{Sin}x,\ y = \text{Sin}2x,\ y = \text{Sin}\tfrac{1}{2}\,x,$$
$$y = 2\text{Sin}2x,\ y = 2\text{Sin}\tfrac{1}{2}\,x,\ y = \tfrac{1}{2}\,\text{Sin}2x,\ y = \tfrac{1}{2}\,\text{Sin}\tfrac{1}{2}\,x$$

Once a collection of graphs has been produced and displayed, it can form the basis of a discussion about the similarities and the differences between the graphs. The main intention is to develop students' understanding of how the period and the amplitude of the different trigonometric functions compare.

This strategy of asking students to produce information for a whole-class discussion by creating an instant display can be applied to most or all areas of the mathematics curriculum. Other examples are:

- exploring linear and quadratic graphs;
- drawing all the possible cuboids made from a fixed number of plastic cubes;
- writing out all the divisors of the numbers from 1 to 100;
- producing all the possible vectors on a certain size of grid.

The idea behind such 'instant' display work is to draw out relationships within the concept under consideration. The main issue here though is about cutting down on marking. Because students are producing work for display, they are not producing work I must use valuable time to mark.

Student presentations

If students come to expect that they will present some aspect of mathematics to their peers, and at the same time learn to listen to each other, presentations can become a powerful aspect of disseminating and learning mathematics. Students can give presentations individually or in small groups. Leading up to a presentation, students might make a poster or produce an OHT about what they have learnt. While presentations might usually be seen as the culmination of a topic, this need not always be the case. For example, if on the spur of the moment I notice a student has, perhaps for the first time, understood a concept which other students may benefit from hearing, he or she could be encouraged to give a short explanation to demonstrate this new-found understanding. For instance, asking a student to explain the convention for rounding up to two-decimal places could be an off-the-cuff presentation and, when handled sensitively, helps develop confidence.

Students setting and marking tests for each other

Imagine a scenario where you have been working with a Year 10 class for, say, three weeks on the central concept of Pythagoras' theorem. Now consider the following:

233

1. Ask pairs of students who usually work at the same pace and achieve similar levels of understanding to write test questions for each other – say three or four questions that will last for approximately 30 minutes.
2. Each student works out answers and prepares a mark scheme. The teacher's role during this part of the process is to check the kind of questions produced and monitor them for comprehension and fairness.
3. At the beginning of the next lesson, students do each other's test questions.
4. At the end of the test students swap papers and, using their prepared mark schemes, mark each other's answers.

Not only are students learning how to answer questions on a specific concept area, they are also learning how to ask, write and mark questions. This is valuable preparation for doing examinations in a more formal setting. Furthermore, because we learn by asking questions as well as knowing how to answer them, this process is valuable; if students can pose questions about a concept, this must mean they have an idea of what the concept is about. Such a process does require the teacher to observe and record what happens, but does not require the teacher to take any marking home.

Experiential learning ... or further ideas for use in classrooms that won't generate 'traditional' quantities of marking

As teachers, we may feel under some pressure not only to provide learning experiences for students, but also to ensure they have something written down in an exercise book, perhaps to demonstrate, make a record of or to prove that they have been 'doing something'. Of course, if students write something in an exercise book it is beholden upon the teacher to demonstrate they have acknowledged this act and offered some response – that is, to show that they have marked it. However, in reality, the majority of our experiences are not something we continually write some kind of record of or commit to paper. People do choose to write diaries, keep records, write letters to friends and make lists such as 'things to do' or 'things to buy' (lists which you then, if you're anything like me, find you've left at home). Professionally, some people engage in reflective practice. Yet as someone who often writes reflective notes about lessons I teach, I could only claim to have written about a very small percentage of the 20,000 odd lessons I have taught over the past 30 years.

There are many opportunities for students to experience mathematics without needing to write about that experience or to do an exercise to show that they have worked on a particular concept. The kind of tasks I refer to are people math situations and those involving the use of practical equipment (I develop these ideas in Chapters 4 and 5). Using such tasks again does not require student to do exercises or write down a lot of information, and this inevitably means they do not create a lot of marking.

I am mindful in writing this chapter that I may appear critical both of the kinds of practices that occur in some schools and of the underlying reasons for such practices. However, my main intention is to consider different ways that teachers might be able to operate in terms of marking and feedback, the nature of planning and the kind of homework tasks set for students. If we spend too much time doing tick/kiss marking we cannot spend sufficient time planning interesting lessons. Planning interesting lessons has an impact upon how students perceive mathematics. The more interested our students are by what we plan for them to do, the better they are likely to respond; the better they respond, the more they will learn and understand; the more they understand, the better they are going to behave ... *everything is connected*.

In this chapter I consider one of the most complex and omnipotent issues regarding how children experience mathematics. It is something where everything becomes connected, and refers to how children are grouped in order to learn mathematics. Specifically, I raise questions about how and why decisions are taken to form separate teaching groups according to notions of students' 'ability'. I strongly and unequivocally argue that by actively deciding not to create so-called ability groups and instead making positive decisions to teach all children in non-setted or mixed-ability groups, we can best help *all* the buggers to add up.

The power of expectation and the dangers of comparison

At the heart of human endeavour is the all-encompassing effect that expectation, both by self and by others, has upon achievement. Self-expectation is fundamental to how we gauge our present accomplishments and the targets we set ourselves for future aspirations and goals. This is true whether we are in a learning situation, digging the garden, writing or going for a jog. A couple of years ago I 'lurched' around the Fairfield Horseshoe in the Lake District in a most disappointing time by comparison to times I had previously achieved. One week later I did the same route and this time knocked 20 minutes off. On each occasion I had expectations of how long it should take, and each time I set myself targets to aspire to. Crucial to my experience and enjoyment of 'running' on the fells is the motivation resulting from targets I set myself, as well as the beauty of being out in the hills. Were I trying to compete against some of those 'maniacal' fell-runners who complete the course in unbelievable times I would probably stay at home and get out a jigsaw; comparing myself to such athletes would be nonsensical. However, I gain inordinate pleasure from what I can achieve; what is important here is not to compare myself to others, and certainly not to concern myself with comparisons made *by* others. I can do nothing about comparisons other people may choose to make.

In classrooms, teachers form expectations of students' achievements. How a teacher transmits these expectations will impact upon the image children form about themselves, and upon their achievement. If the culture of a classroom is about children not being compared to each other then we can set up useful forms of competition based upon children competing with their personal best. In such a culture, targets are negotiated and agreed between the individual child and the teacher; expectations can be challenging yet realistic. Creating situations that cause children to compare themselves with each other is to detract from the more important business of personal achievement. Of course, children do compare themselves to one another and soon find out who is the fastest, the cleverest, the wittiest, the richest and the poorest: but as adults we don't have to subscribe to this, or encourage it.

By creating ability sets we are, however, creating a potentially damaging culture based upon comparison. Children inevitably form opinions about what expectations they believe their teachers have of them; the set a child is placed in sends 'clear' messages about what these are. Whether we encourage it not, or like it or not, children talk about the 'dumbos' in the low sets and the 'swots' in the high sets. Yet we cannot separate out emotional factors of learning from cognitive aspects of learning: how we feel about what we do impacts upon the quality of the outcomes we achieve. Suffice to say, if children constantly receive subliminal messages about how 'good' or how 'weak' they are, according to the set number they are allocated, this will directly impact upon their responses and behaviour in the present and achievements in the future.

I have considerable experience of teaching mathematics in both setted and non-setted groups. These experiences lead me to the strong conviction that not only is the latter by far the most rewarding and intellectually challenging way to teach mathematics, it is also the most mathematically enabling and socially just form of organization within which children learn mathematics. Learning in non-setted teaching groups is an issue of inclusion. In this final chapter I make a strong case, from a practitioner's perspective, for teaching mathematics without placing children in so-called 'ability groups'.

I have also experienced the ignominy of being taught in a bottom stream myself between the ages of 11 and 14 and, therefore, have a good angle on what this feels like. As an adult I can articulate what impact this experience had upon my self-esteem. I do not need theories or research data to understand what being in the bottom set is like, I know what it's like and it's not nice. I also know what it is like to have to gain self-respect amongst my peers by being expert at being 'bad', that gaining kudos when academic avenues had been cut off meant finding other, non-academic ways of showing my 'worth'. How I subsequently managed to 'aspire' to become a teacher, a head of mathematics and a senior lecturer is unimportant. What is important is that I am one of a small minority of mathematics teachers who has personally experienced what being in the 'bottom' mathematics class is like. I therefore speak with some authority and much insight.

Developing my self-esteem as a 14 year old 'mathematician'

How we help students develop their self-esteem in mathematics is clearly an important consideration. How students in 'bottom' sets, however, are helped to build their self-esteem is a highly complex issue, particularly if the very system of setting has the potential to create groups of youngsters who have a high degree of low-esteem. This was certainly the case for myself as a 14-year-old, when I was provided with a diet of very boring mathematics that was a replication of the kind of work I had done in my primary years and continued to do into my 3rd year (or Year 9 in new money). One day, however, for some reason which I could not understand at the time, my mathematics teacher, who was actually a P.E. teacher who taught the Year 9 bottom set for mathematics, taught the class something markedly different from the kind of mathematics we had previously been used to: solving simultaneous equations.

I didn't know why I was solving these equations or what they were for, but I knew this 'algebra' work, which involved xs and ys, was what pupils in the top set did. I therefore felt to be doing something *really* important. Discovering I was capable of doing the kind of work other pupils in higher sets were doing was a significant realization and a significant boost to my self-esteem. Furthermore, I could use algebra to check my answers and know whether I had worked them out correctly; I remember the power of being able to do some *really hard* maths. That evening, quite voluntarily, I solved 50 or 60 simultaneous equations, filling page after page of my exercise book with their solutions. The next day I could barely wait for the maths lesson to begin so I could show Mr Green what I had achieved. I was bursting with pride.

Upon deeper reflection, it was Mr Green who provided me with access to mathematics; he was the person who offered me the joy of real success and the confidence to feel I could do mathematics. I had achieved success at a level beyond the expectations of myself and my teachers. I firmly believe this event had a profound impact upon my development; this, perhaps, was my first encounter with the entitlement curriculum.

Setting, social class and politics

Setting students by measures of perceived 'ability', as a form of creating teaching groups, mirrors some aspects of our UK society. These are the class distinctions that pervade daily life, in some shape or other, and impact upon so much of potential causes of inequality. That a class system exists cannot be denied. In his article in the *TES*, 'Little improvement in the lot of the poor' (29 April 2005), Peter Wilby (editor of the *New Statesman*) offered the following: '... for compulsory education, the biggest policy priority should be to create, in each school, a mix of abilities and home backgrounds that comes as close as possible to the mix in the general population.' This is a timely suggestion, and whether this system needs to be perpetuated in our schools in the guise of students' needs and how best they can be provided for, through setting by ability, is something teachers can decide to do something about.

Sukhnandan and Lee (1988, 43) in their review of research, offer the following: '... homogeneous forms of grouping reinforce segregation of pupils in terms of social class gender, race and age (season of birth). Consequently, low ability classes often contain a disproportionately large number of pupils from working-class backgrounds, boys, ethnic minorities and summer-born children.' Mirroring forms of elitism in terms of class, gender, race and age can surely not be considered a humanitarian basis for our mathematical education system, yet one has to look far and wide to find many mathematics departments teaching in mixed-attainment groups beyond Year 7. I was interested to hear Mike Askew (Professor of Education, King's College, London) in his closing speech to delegates at the 6th British Congress of Mathematics Education (BCME) conference (University of Warwick, 30 March–2 April 2005). Mike frequently gave support to mixed-attainment teaching, noting that in Finland grouping by ability was abolished 20 years ago. Indeed, the Finnish system of education was given further praise in a study into pupil performance across 40 counties by the Organisation for Economic Co-operation and Development (OECD). 'Finland was the undisputed winner,' noted Warwick Mansell in the *TES* (6 May 2005). Mansell went on to say: 'There is little setting or streaming. Even in subjects such as maths, where differences in pupils' capabilities can be great, the philosophy is to educate children in all-ability classrooms.' This issue of there being wide differences in students' mathematical capabilities is one which, I suggest, is the root cause behind decisions to create 'ability' groups. Yet the preponderance to ignore the fact that all groups of pupils have wide variations of cognition and attainment in them is disingenuous. Give a class an accessible problem to work on, have loads of extension tasks sprinkled liberally around the classroom, find appropriate challenges, and we will find setting can be consigned to the dustbin of educational theory.

However, education has been the constant focus of both Labour and Conservative governments since the Callaghan 'Ruskin' lecture in 1976. Recently the 'one size fits all' mantra has been used to criticize the basis of comprehensive education.

Furthermore, setting by 'ability' was strongly encouraged by the 1997 Labour government; for example, in their White Paper, *Excellence in Schools* (July 1997), where setting was advocated by the following: 'setting pupils according to ability ... as one way of modernising the comprehensive principle.' In 2000, in a leaked Labour Policy Forum document (the *Guardian*, 27 May 2000), the following appeared: 'We want to see schools which focus on what works and abandon any residual dogmatic attachment to mixed-ability teaching.' The language of 'what works' seems to suggest this idea is 'common sense': however, for thousands of children who experience a bottom set curriculum and who consequently have bottom set expectations, setting may not necessarily feel to be something that 'works' or something that makes sense to them. (Ollerton (2001) *Support for Learning*)

At this point I invite readers to hum the tune of 'The William Tell overture'. This is because there is, potentially, a saviour in our midst in the form of Ofsted. In both the 2004 and 2005 subject study reports (into mathematics) the following quotes appear:

- Too many pupils begin a course aimed at the foundation tier of entry for GCSE, which is limited in nature and ambition, rather than continuing with a broader teaching programme until a later decision about GCSE entry can be made (2004).
- At the start of Key Stage 4, some pupils who have not achieved as well as they had hoped in Key Stage 3 tests have negative views about mathematics. The subsequent teaching in Key Stage 4 too often fails to inspire these pupils and their self-confidence continues to decline (2004).
- Inflexible setting arrangements in Key Stage 4 lead many pupils to believe that their GCSE goals in mathematics are limited in nature and ambition. Many become disaffected and choose to channel their energy and enthusiasm into other subject areas in which they believe they will achieve better results (2005).

Each of these quotes suggest a growing recognition that setting might not be all it is cracked up to be. If through inflexible setting arrangements we create a situation of significant numbers of students who write off their chances of achieving the holy grail of at least a grade C at GCSE, perhaps we should not be surprised if some of these students find other ways of gaining kudos. This can and does happen and leads to disillusionment, frequently manifested in poor behaviour and attendance, creating difficulties for teachers and fellow students alike.

At my last school we operated a modular, problem-solving, accessible starting-point, extension-task curriculum model. This meant we did not have to determine which tier of GCSE examination students would be entered for until such information had to be sent to the exam board. From the end of January onwards, in Year 11, we just practised going through past paper after past paper. This approach was quite a novel one for students, yet because we all recognized we were just playing the examination 'game', and because this was (and continues to be) the currency students must have, the approach seemed to 'work'. Interestingly enough, and possibly because we had worked on students developing personal responsibility, it was unproblematic to have students working on all three tiers of paper in the same lesson. Answers to the papers were freely available and this meant students could identify personal targets and revision needs, and choose to seek help when necessary. In mixed attainment groups Year 11 students quite naturally asked one another for help, having been encouraged to work in this way from the beginning of Year 7. Given that teaching something is the most powerful way of learning something, and deepening one's understanding of a process or of a concept, then having students teach each other is a fundamentally important strategy. I develop this issue on pages 248–9.

Above all is the issue of students' dignity and self-esteem. If students in 'top' sets are sometimes referred to as 'the cream', what does this say about those in the 'bottom' set? Giving every student 'top' set learning opportunities, so all students can experience mathematics in ways which enables them to do their best with what is on offer, rather than some being offered a restricted mathematical diet, is fundamental to mixed-attainment grouping.

Teaching in mixed-ability groups ... 'Well, we wouldn't do it any other way'

The last secondary school mathematics department I taught in did not group students by ability and we rarely used textbooks. We developed a range of strategies and used a lot of equipment and problem-solving approaches to teach mathematics. We also had a lot of visitors. On one occasion a colleague was being quizzed during morning break by a group of visitors about how it was possible to teach mathematics in mixed-ability groups. His response was: 'Well, we wouldn't do it any other way.'

At the time, this was interesting because as a department we had evolved from teaching mathematics in setted groups to non-setted groups, year by year, over a four-year period. Part of this process involved the use of departmental meetings to share ideas for the classroom and to evaluate how our teaching in non-setted groups was progressing. Teaching in non-setted groups became the most obvious and normal way to teach mathematics, and having started to develop a departmental pedagogy, we would not think about teaching any other way. We looked at starting points and discussed extension tasks, shared concerns and considered what was working well. As such, we engaged in a massive amount of in-house professional and curriculum development. Working towards teaching in non-setted groups was, therefore, the driving force behind many developments, where everything became connected: strategies, resources, schemes of work, methods of assessment, furniture arrangements, improvements in GCSE results and, by comparison to subjects taught in 'ability' groups, better behaved students in our classrooms. One reason for this better behaviour was because we worked with individuals to help them achieve their best, and did not have notional targets according to the set number students were allocated.

Difficulties with differentiation

Afars, Bilen, Dedareb, Kunama, Nara, Rashaida, Saho, Tigre, Tigrinya. Our nine ethnic groups each bring different gifts to enrich Eritrea. As diverse as we are, we are united in one purpose – making a peaceful, prosperous country.

These words were engraved in a two-metre high glass panel exhibit in 'Expo 2001' in Asmara, Eritrea. There is a strong sense here of not just coping with diversity, but using it to the benefit of all. There is, I believe, an incontrovertible argument that teaching mathematics with diverse groups of students is not just something that is worth doing on social justice grounds, it is also a way of raising standards and benefiting every child's learning potential.

The most common reason I hear for creating 'ability' groups is to minimize the ability range, thus enabling teachers to 'target' their teaching at an appropriate level and to 'sort out' difficulties with differentiation. Such reasons, however, deny or fail to take into account the 'fact' that in any class there are as many different levels of attainment as there are children in the room. Even in the most tightly setted group a range of attainment exists: in one school I visited, the 'lowest' set number went as far as 13. Just imagine being taught in set 13 out of 13.

Working with differentiation is complex – but then so is teaching. To attempt to avoid wide variations of differentiation is to simplify what cannot be simplified: the complexity of teaching 30 individual children. If setting is used to try to make differentiation easier, then dangers exist of teaching to a specific level: yet the notion of 'a' level does not exist; it never has done and never will do. Planning lessons in ways that acknowledge and seek to accommodate differentiation is at the heart of effective teaching and 'natural' learning. As such, it is imperative to look at methods of structuring teaching which embrace differentiation rather than creating structural and organizational edifices to overcome difficulties with it. The issue in non-setted classrooms has nothing to do with minimizing the range and has everything to do with maximizing opportunities for working with students' differences ... and *differences are normal.*

Two key issues to consider when working with groups of children with wide-ranging aspirations, motivations, current attainments and future achievements are:

- constructing modules of ideas to offer a fresh start;
- developing a range of teaching strategies.

Fresh start

I have already discussed in some detail the model of constructing modules based upon accessible, rich starting points, and devising a range of extension tasks. This model is based on helping individuals to find their own 'level' in order to help them develop their mathematical thinking. A significant issue from students' perspective is that each module offers a fresh-start opportunity. So, no matter what anyone has achieved in the past, anyone can achieve differently in the future. This is the basis of inclusion and self-determination. 'Levels' do not need to be assigned to individual performance because, unremarkably, human nature does not countenance the notion that human beings operate at a certain fixed or predicted level. In reality we shift between levels of cognition, sometimes failing to see the most obvious idea staring us in the face, while at other times making an intuitive leap and finding a solution to a problem when we least expected to. Indeed, on one occasion, I remember waking up in the middle of the night with the solution to a problem I had been working and getting stuck on from an Open University course. So vivid was the solution I had to write it down there and then in case the memory evaded me in the morning. This was certainly an amazing event: however, it confirmed to me the power of one's mind and its capability of operating at highly sophisticated levels even when the rest of the person lay sleeping.

Having a fresh start at the beginning of each module means past achievements do not predict future accomplishments. To help students realize their potential and develop their mathematical thinking, teachers need to develop a wide range of strategies. Access is the key.

I align to the notion of a fresh start the phrase 'hope springs eternal' and, as a Shrewsbury Town fan, this phrase has a ring of truth; certainly for the 3,000 fans who turn up game after game in the hope that a new dawn is just round the corner. The phrase was even more salient as a fan in the Ataturk stadium with Liverpool 3–0 down to Milan at half time. Children in classrooms must also be encouraged to recognize that they are never a 'lost cause' and that opportunities to achieve and to make sense of concepts which may initially appear insurmountable are always feasible. To help students work from such an optimistic perspective, they must be encouraged to inhabit mindsets of being able to overcome barriers to learning. Expectations of self and of their teachers play a significant part here; experiencing mathematics in classes which are not based upon students' measured 'ability' is fundamental to raising their self-worth and realistic expectations.

Developing a range of teaching strategies

One of the more amazing features of our departmental shift towards teaching in non-setted groups was the wide range of strategies we developed to cater for different students' attainments. This did not mean we attempted to construct individual learning packages, nor did we use an individualized mathematics scheme based upon hundreds of workcards. We did, however, amass many strategies and use a range of resources.

To introduce a planned extension task for the first time during a module, I would temporarily gather together those students who I felt were, or soon would be, ready to work on a further idea, and work with this group for the next few minutes. Subsequently, as I sensed more students were ready to extend their thinking, I might ask a student who had already begun this task to temporarily take on the mantle of 'teacher'. Asking students to explain ideas to one another is both a valuable teaching resource and a powerful way of helping students deepen their knowledge.

If during a module one student became 'stuck', I would frequently suggest this person talk to another, whom I was confident could provide help. An important aspect of this strategy was that it was not always higher attaining, more confident students who helped their lower attaining peers.

Sometimes quite the reverse happened. For example, on one occasion I asked a student who had a statement of special educational need (and who 'loved' computers) to explain to a student destined for a high grade at GCSE (and who claimed to 'hate' computers) how to use a dynamic geometry program. What was interesting about this particular interaction was the higher attaining student recognized I had another agenda, which was about boosting the SEN student's self-esteem. She was absolutely right and we both knew it!

The ebb and flow of an inclusive classroom

Throughout lessons, therefore, different students would work together, possibly going back to their chosen work place or sometimes choosing to stay together for the remainder of a lesson. When students expect such movement to take place, the rhythm of a lesson is very much one of ebb and flow. This is the stuff of classrooms. To recognize the web of relationships that exists between teacher, students and mathematics means using one's own relationships with mathematics and with students to help them forge a stronger, more confident relationship with mathematics. We do not need to label who are the high achievers and who struggle; we will find this out quickly enough, but such perceptions cannot remain fixed. If we stick rigidly to any judgements we make and use this information to form different 'ability' groups, then we attribute ourselves with powers and responsibilities we have no right to claim.

There's a lovely quote from Bishop Desmond Tutu: 'Without all the colours there would be no rainbow.' To create a rainbow of achievement and provide opportunities for all children to become confident, to find ways of helping them all make sense of *the* most abstract discipline, to 'shine' mathematically, requires them to be included. The more the kids shine, the more we get out of our teaching. Finding ways of including everyone to learn mathematics without separation or segregation is to help all the buggers add up.

Bibliography

ATM (1989) *Points of Departure 3*, Phelan Printers, Derby.

Banwell, C., Saunders, K. and Tahta, D. (1972) *Starting Points*, Tarquin, Norfolk (out of print).

Black, P., and Wiliam, D., (1998) *Inside the black box*.

Bloomfield, A. (1990) *People Maths*, Stanley Thorne, Cheltenham.

Cockcroft, W. (1982) *Mathematics Counts*; Report of inquiry into teaching mathematics in schools, London, HMSO.

Cooper, B., and Dunne, M., (2000) *Assessing children's mathematical knowledge: Social class, Sex and problem solving*, Buckingham, Open University Press.

Courant, R. and Robbins, H. (1941) *What is Mathematics*, Oxford University Press, Oxford.

Cundy, H. M. and Rollett, A. P. (1952) *Mathematical Models*, Oxford University Press, Oxford.

DES (1985) *Mathematics from 5 to 16*, HMSO, London.

HMI (2004) Ofsted Subject reports 2002/03. Mathematics in Secondary Schools, www.ofsted.gov.uk.

HMI (2005) Ofsted Subject reports 2003/04. Mathematics in Secondary Schools, www.ofsted.gov.uk.

Lacey, P. (1998) 'Using geometric images of number to teach mental addition and subtraction.' *Mathematics Teaching* 163, ATM, Derby.

Moon, B. and Shelton-Mayes, A. (eds) (1994) *Teaching and Learning in the Secondary School*, Routledge, London.

Morgan, C., and Watson, A., (2002) 'The interpretive nature of teachers' assessment of students' mathematics: issues for equity'. *Journal for Research into Mathematics Education*.

Ollerton, M. (2001) Inclusion and entitlement, equality of

    opportunity and quality of curriculum provision. *Support for Learning*, Vol. 16, No. 1.

Ollerton, M. (2002) *Learning and teaching mathematics without a textbook*, ATM, Derby.

Ollerton, M. (2003) *Creating positive classrooms*, Continuum, London.

Ollerton, M. (2005) *100 Ideas for Teaching Mathematics*, Continuum, London.

Ollerton, M. and Watson, A. (2001) *Inclusive Mathematics 11–18*, Continuum, London.

Pirsig, R. (1976) *Zen and the art of motorcycle maintenance*, Corgi, Transworld Publishers.

Postman, N. and Weingartner, C. (1971) *Teaching as a Subversive Activity*. Penguin: London.

Reichmann, W. J. (1967) *The spell of mathematics*, Penguin, England & Australia.

Smith, A. (2004) *Making mathematics count*. Department for Education and Skills: London.

Sotto, E. (1994) *When teaching becomes learning: A theory and practice of teaching*, Cassell, London.

Sukhnandan, L. with Lee, B. (1998) 'Streaming, setting and grouping by ability: a review of the literature', NFER.

Watson, A. and Mason, M. (1998) *Questions and prompts for mathematical thinking*, ATM, Derby.

Index